NIV

once a·day

31

DAYS OF WISDOM

D1414794

ZONDERVAN®

Walk Thru the Bible

CONTENTS

DEDICATION

To Rob Price (1961–2011)

A remarkable encourager, a loyal friend and a humble servant of God at Walk Thru the Bible for almost two decades.

"Trust in the LORD with all your heart and lean not on your own understanding; in all your ways submit to him, and he will make your paths straight." —*Proverbs 3:5–6*

ABOUT WALK THRU THE BIBLE

For more than three decades, Walk Thru the Bible has been dedicated to igniting a passion for God's Word worldwide through live events, devotional magazines, and resources designed for both small groups and individual use. Known for innovative methods and high-quality resources, we serve the whole body of Christ across denominational, cultural and national lines.

Walk Thru the Bible communicates the truths of God's Word in a way that makes the Bible readily accessible to anyone. We are committed to developing user-friendly resources that are Bible centered, of excellent quality, life changing for individuals, and catalytic for churches, ministries and movements; and we are committed to maintaining our global reach through strategic partnerships while adhering to the highest levels of integrity in all we do.

Walk Thru the Bible partners with the local church worldwide to fulfill its mission, helping people "walk thru" the Bible with greater clarity and understanding. Live events and small group curricula are taught in over 45 languages by more than 30,000 instructors in more than 104 countries, and more than 100 million devotionals have been packaged into daily magazines, books and other publications that reach over 5 million people each year.

Walk Thru the Bible
www.walkthru.org
1-800-361-6131

CONTRIBUTORS TO
NIV ONCE-A-DAY 31 DAYS OF WISDOM

Chris Tiegreen, Editor

day1

Purpose and Theme

1 The proverbs of Solomon son of David, king of Israel:

² for gaining wisdom and instruction;
    for understanding words of insight;
³ for receiving instruction in prudent behavior,
    doing what is right and just and fair;
⁴ for giving prudence to those who are simple,ᵃ
    knowledge and discretion to the young—
⁵ let the wise listen and add to their learning,
    and let the discerning get guidance—
⁶ for understanding proverbs and parables,
    the sayings and riddles of the wise.ᵇ

⁷ The fear of the LORD is the beginning of knowledge,
    but foolsᶜ despise wisdom and instruction.

Prologue: Exhortations to Embrace Wisdom

Warning Against the Invitation of Sinful Men

⁸ Listen, my son, to your father's instruction
    and do not forsake your mother's teaching.
⁹ They are a garland to grace your head
    and a chain to adorn your neck.

¹⁰ My son, if sinful men entice you,
    do not give in to them.
¹¹ If they say, "Come along with us;
    let's lie in wait for innocent blood,
    let's ambush some harmless soul;

ᵃ 4 The Hebrew word rendered *simple* in Proverbs denotes a person who is gullible, without moral direction and inclined to evil.   ᵇ 6 Or *understanding a proverb, namely, a parable, / and the sayings of the wise, their riddles*
ᶜ 7 The Hebrew words rendered *fool* in Proverbs, and often elsewhere in the Old Testament, denote a person who is morally deficient.

¹²let's swallow them alive, like the grave,
    and whole, like those who go down to the pit;
¹³we will get all sorts of valuable things
    and fill our houses with plunder;
¹⁴cast lots with us;
    we will all share the loot"—
¹⁵my son, do not go along with them,
    do not set foot on their paths;
¹⁶for their feet rush into evil,
    they are swift to shed blood.
¹⁷How useless to spread a net
    where every bird can see it!
¹⁸These men lie in wait for their own blood;
    they ambush only themselves!
¹⁹Such are the paths of all who go after ill-gotten gain;
    it takes away the life of those who get it.

Wisdom's Rebuke

²⁰Out in the open wisdom calls aloud,
    she raises her voice in the public square;
²¹on top of the wall*a* she cries out,
    at the city gate she makes her speech:

²²"How long will you who are simple love your simple ways?
    How long will mockers delight in mockery
    and fools hate knowledge?
²³Repent at my rebuke!
    Then I will pour out my thoughts to you,
    I will make known to you my teachings.
²⁴But since you refuse to listen when I call
    and no one pays attention when I stretch out my hand,
²⁵since you disregard all my advice
    and do not accept my rebuke,
²⁶I in turn will laugh when disaster strikes you;
    I will mock when calamity overtakes you—
²⁷when calamity overtakes you like a storm,
    when disaster sweeps over you like a whirlwind,
    when distress and trouble overwhelm you.

---

a 21 Septuagint; Hebrew / *at noisy street corners*

[28] "Then they will call to me but I will not answer;
   they will look for me but will not find me,
[29] since they hated knowledge
   and did not choose to fear the LORD.
[30] Since they would not accept my advice
   and spurned my rebuke,
[31] they will eat the fruit of their ways
   and be filled with the fruit of their schemes.
[32] For the waywardness of the simple will kill them,
   and the complacency of fools will destroy them;
[33] but whoever listens to me will live in safety
   and be at ease, without fear of harm."

REFLECTION

on PROVERBS 1:1–7

The purpose of the book of Proverbs is spelled out in its first few verses. Those who read it and heed it will gain wisdom, understanding, insight and the knowledge of what is right, just and fair. These words are helpful for all people—old and especially the young, sages and simpletons, the experienced and the naive. This is a collection of really good advice.

When reading the proverbs, it's important to recognize that they describe how God designed life to work. They don't necessarily represent the spiritual equivalent of the law of gravity: hard-and-fast commands and promises that apply to all situations. For example, Proverbs 3:1–2 and 4:10 trumpet the power of wise instruction to produce prosperity and long life for those who follow the advice. We know from other portions of Scripture, however, that disaster and death can strike a godly person. So while such statements generally are true, the individual proverbs are not to be interpreted as prophetic guarantees of cause and effect.   ❧

day2

Moral Benefits of Wisdom

2 My son, if you accept my words
   and store up my commands within you,
² turning your ear to wisdom
   and applying your heart to understanding—
³ indeed, if you call out for insight
   and cry aloud for understanding,
⁴ and if you look for it as for silver
   and search for it as for hidden treasure,
⁵ then you will understand the fear of the LORD
   and find the knowledge of God.
⁶ For the LORD gives wisdom;
   from his mouth come knowledge and understanding.
⁷ He holds success in store for the upright,
   he is a shield to those whose walk is blameless,
⁸ for he guards the course of the just
   and protects the way of his faithful ones.

⁹ Then you will understand what is right and just
   and fair—every good path.
¹⁰ For wisdom will enter your heart,
   and knowledge will be pleasant to your soul.
¹¹ Discretion will protect you,
   and understanding will guard you.

¹² Wisdom will save you from the ways of wicked men,
   from men whose words are perverse,
¹³ who have left the straight paths
   to walk in dark ways,
¹⁴ who delight in doing wrong
   and rejoice in the perverseness of evil,
¹⁵ whose paths are crooked
   and who are devious in their ways.

¹⁶ Wisdom will save you also from the adulterous woman,
   from the wayward woman with her seductive words,

¹⁷ who has left the partner of her youth
    and ignored the covenant she made before God.^a
¹⁸ Surely her house leads down to death
    and her paths to the spirits of the dead.
¹⁹ None who go to her return
    or attain the paths of life.

²⁰ Thus you will walk in the ways of the good
    and keep to the paths of the righteous.
²¹ For the upright will live in the land,
    and the blameless will remain in it;
²² but the wicked will be cut off from the land,
    and the unfaithful will be torn from it.

^a 17 Or *covenant of her God*

REFLECTION

on **PROVERBS 2:1–6**

Wisdom doesn't just come to us. We don't get it through osmosis or passivity or a moment of enlightenment. We have to search for understanding as for hidden treasure, and that's a lifelong process. One of the most important things we can do is described in verse 3: Ask for it. That's how Solomon acquired his wisdom (see 1 Kings 3:5–9), and that's how we get almost anything of importance in life. We pray, asking God for what only he can give.

The assurance of an answer is given in Proverbs 2:6. We don't pray to a silent God. He gives understanding. In the New Testament, we are told that believers in Jesus have his mind (1 Corinthians 2:16) and that God grants wisdom freely to those who ask and believe (James 1:5–6). Those who seek understanding from God will receive it—over time, through diligence and persistence, in the context of a relationship with him. If we want to be wise, we have to draw close to the source of all wisdom.   ❖

day3

Wisdom Bestows Well-Being

3 My son, do not forget my teaching,
  but keep my commands in your heart,
² for they will prolong your life many years
  and bring you peace and prosperity.

³ Let love and faithfulness never leave you;
  bind them around your neck,
  write them on the tablet of your heart.
⁴ Then you will win favor and a good name
  in the sight of God and man.

⁵ Trust in the LORD with all your heart
  and lean not on your own understanding;
⁶ in all your ways submit to him,
  and he will make your paths straight.*ᵃ*

⁷ Do not be wise in your own eyes;
  fear the LORD and shun evil.
⁸ This will bring health to your body
  and nourishment to your bones.

⁹ Honor the LORD with your wealth,
  with the firstfruits of all your crops;
¹⁰ then your barns will be filled to overflowing,
  and your vats will brim over with new wine.

¹¹ My son, do not despise the LORD's discipline,
  and do not resent his rebuke,
¹² because the LORD disciplines those he loves,
  as a father the son he delights in.*ᵇ*

¹³ Blessed are those who find wisdom,
  those who gain understanding,
¹⁴ for she is more profitable than silver
  and yields better returns than gold.

ᵃ 6 Or *will direct your paths*   *ᵇ 12* Hebrew; Septuagint *loves, / and he chastens everyone he accepts as his child*

¹⁵ She is more precious than rubies;
     nothing you desire can compare with her.
¹⁶ Long life is in her right hand;
     in her left hand are riches and honor.
¹⁷ Her ways are pleasant ways,
     and all her paths are peace.
¹⁸ She is a tree of life to those who take hold of her;
     those who hold her fast will be blessed.

¹⁹ By wisdom the Lord laid the earth's foundations,
     by understanding he set the heavens in place;
²⁰ by his knowledge the watery depths were divided,
     and the clouds let drop the dew.

²¹ My son, do not let wisdom and understanding out of your
          sight,
     preserve sound judgment and discretion;
²² they will be life for you,
     an ornament to grace your neck.
²³ Then you will go on your way in safety,
     and your foot will not stumble.
²⁴ When you lie down, you will not be afraid;
     when you lie down, your sleep will be sweet.
²⁵ Have no fear of sudden disaster
     or of the ruin that overtakes the wicked,
²⁶ for the Lord will be at your side
     and will keep your foot from being snared.

²⁷ Do not withhold good from those to whom it is due,
     when it is in your power to act.
²⁸ Do not say to your neighbor,
     "Come back tomorrow and I'll give it to you"—
     when you already have it with you.
²⁹ Do not plot harm against your neighbor,
     who lives trustfully near you.
³⁰ Do not accuse anyone for no reason—
     when they have done you no harm.

³¹ Do not envy the violent
     or choose any of their ways.

³² For the Lord detests the perverse
     but takes the upright into his confidence.

[33] The LORD's curse is on the house of the wicked,
   but he blesses the home of the righteous.
[34] He mocks proud mockers
   but shows favor to the humble and oppressed.
[35] The wise inherit honor,
   but fools get only shame.

REFLECTION

on **PROVERBS 3:5–6**

Solomon's father, David, urged him to serve the Lord with whole-hearted devotion (see 1 Chronicles 28:9). Now Solomon, likely the author of most of Proverbs, passes the same advice on to his own sons. These rich, well-known verses tell us to trust in God with all our heart—to lean on the understanding of the one who has a truly accurate perspective and a clear view of the past, present and future.

It makes much more sense to depend on the infinite mind of all wisdom and knowledge rather than on our own finite minds. Yet, perhaps from fear that we won't be able to access his wisdom, we often lean on our own understanding. We list pros and cons, project as many possible outcomes as we can think of and obsess about details we can't control. But if we disavow our own wisdom and truly lean on the promise God gives us, submitting entirely to him, he will direct our paths—even when those paths appear random. He knows how to get his children where we need to go. ❖

day4

Get Wisdom at Any Cost

4 Listen, my sons, to a father's instruction;
  pay attention and gain understanding.
[2] I give you sound learning,
  so do not forsake my teaching.
[3] For I too was a son to my father,
  still tender, and cherished by my mother.
[4] Then he taught me, and he said to me,
  "Take hold of my words with all your heart;
  keep my commands, and you will live.
[5] Get wisdom, get understanding;
  do not forget my words or turn away from them.
[6] Do not forsake wisdom, and she will protect you;
  love her, and she will watch over you.
[7] The beginning of wisdom is this: Get[a] wisdom.
  Though it cost all you have,[b] get understanding.
[8] Cherish her, and she will exalt you;
  embrace her, and she will honor you.
[9] She will give you a garland to grace your head
  and present you with a glorious crown."

[10] Listen, my son, accept what I say,
  and the years of your life will be many.
[11] I instruct you in the way of wisdom
  and lead you along straight paths.
[12] When you walk, your steps will not be hampered;
  when you run, you will not stumble.
[13] Hold on to instruction, do not let it go;
  guard it well, for it is your life.
[14] Do not set foot on the path of the wicked
  or walk in the way of evildoers.
[15] Avoid it, do not travel on it;
  turn from it and go on your way.

[a] 7 Or *Wisdom is supreme; therefore get*   [b] 7 Or *wisdom. / Whatever else you get*

¹⁶ For they cannot rest until they do evil;
 they are robbed of sleep till they make someone stumble.
¹⁷ They eat the bread of wickedness
 and drink the wine of violence.

¹⁸ The path of the righteous is like the morning sun,
 shining ever brighter till the full light of day.
¹⁹ But the way of the wicked is like deep darkness;
 they do not know what makes them stumble.

²⁰ My son, pay attention to what I say;
 turn your ear to my words.
²¹ Do not let them out of your sight,
 keep them within your heart;
²² for they are life to those who find them
 and health to one's whole body.
²³ Above all else, guard your heart,
 for everything you do flows from it.
²⁴ Keep your mouth free of perversity;
 keep corrupt talk far from your lips.
²⁵ Let your eyes look straight ahead;
 fix your gaze directly before you.
²⁶ Give careful thought to theᵃ paths for your feet
 and be steadfast in all your ways.
²⁷ Do not turn to the right or the left;
 keep your foot from evil.

ᵃ 26 Or *Make level*

REFLECTION

on **PROVERBS 4:23**

"Above all else." Those are significant words cluing us in to our priority in this whole wisdom adventure. Yes, it's important to fill our minds with truth and seek understanding. We direct our eyes and watch our mouths and take careful steps. But above all, we need to guard our hearts. None of the rest matters if our motives and passions override our thoughts and behaviors. The leanings of our hearts influence how we interpret the wisdom we receive and apply it to our lives.

While we may assume that guarding our hearts is simply a matter of keeping bad things out, it's also important to guard the heart by keeping the good things in. Whatever truth we learn, the seeds that are planted within us by God, the desires that fit his kingdom purposes — these must all be cultivated. Our tendency is to become highly motivated and impacted by the Spirit and then let our motives and determination slowly slip away. Guarding our hearts — keeping negative influences out and positive influences in — points our thoughts and actions in the right direction.   ❖

day5

Warning Against Adultery

5 My son, pay attention to my wisdom,
   turn your ear to my words of insight,
² that you may maintain discretion
   and your lips may preserve knowledge.
³ For the lips of the adulterous woman drip honey,
   and her speech is smoother than oil;
⁴ but in the end she is bitter as gall,
   sharp as a double-edged sword.
⁵ Her feet go down to death;
   her steps lead straight to the grave.
⁶ She gives no thought to the way of life;
   her paths wander aimlessly, but she does not know it.

⁷ Now then, my sons, listen to me;
   do not turn aside from what I say.
⁸ Keep to a path far from her,
   do not go near the door of her house,
⁹ lest you lose your honor to others
   and your dignity[a] to one who is cruel,
¹⁰ lest strangers feast on your wealth
   and your toil enrich the house of another.
¹¹ At the end of your life you will groan,
   when your flesh and body are spent.
¹² You will say, "How I hated discipline!
   How my heart spurned correction!
¹³ I would not obey my teachers
   or turn my ear to my instructors.
¹⁴ And I was soon in serious trouble
   in the assembly of God's people."

¹⁵ Drink water from your own cistern,
   running water from your own well.

[a] 9 Or *years*

16 Should your springs overflow in the streets,
  your streams of water in the public squares?
17 Let them be yours alone,
  never to be shared with strangers.
18 May your fountain be blessed,
  and may you rejoice in the wife of your youth.
19 A loving doe, a graceful deer—
  may her breasts satisfy you always,
  may you ever be intoxicated with her love.
20 Why, my son, be intoxicated with another man's wife?
  Why embrace the bosom of a wayward woman?

21 For your ways are in full view of the LORD,
  and he examines all your paths.
22 The evil deeds of the wicked ensnare them;
  the cords of their sins hold them fast.
23 For lack of discipline they will die,
  led astray by their own great folly.

REFLECTION

on **PROVERBS 5:1–23**

Proverbs contains many warnings against adultery and the seductions of illicit pleasures. These warnings are from a king, surrounded by a multitude of wives and concubines, who had learned quite a few lessons to pass on to his sons—but they have larger spiritual implications too. The greatest law God gave to his people is to love him with everything in them. And the greatest sin throughout Scripture is idolatry—or, as the prophets put it, spiritual adultery. In God's eyes, faithfulness is a really big deal.

Whether a temptation is physical or spiritual, the dynamics are the same. It looks enticing. It may seem harmless. The lips of temptation seem to drip honey and speak soothingly (see verse 3). But life is full of rationales that lead to ruin and promises that lead to pain. God is no enemy of pleasure—he invented it and offers it to us (see Psalm 16:11)—but the enemy and our flesh exploit our desires and aim them in unfulfilling directions. We need to be discerning; any kind of unfaithfulness will leave us empty.   ✤

day6

Warnings Against Folly

6 My son, if you have put up security for your neighbor,
if you have shaken hands in pledge for a stranger,
² you have been trapped by what you said,
ensnared by the words of your mouth.
³ So do this, my son, to free yourself,
since you have fallen into your neighbor's hands:
Go—to the point of exhaustion—*a*
and give your neighbor no rest!
⁴ Allow no sleep to your eyes,
no slumber to your eyelids.
⁵ Free yourself, like a gazelle from the hand of the hunter,
like a bird from the snare of the fowler.

⁶ Go to the ant, you sluggard;
consider its ways and be wise!
⁷ It has no commander,
no overseer or ruler,
⁸ yet it stores its provisions in summer
and gathers its food at harvest.

⁹ How long will you lie there, you sluggard?
When will you get up from your sleep?
¹⁰ A little sleep, a little slumber,
a little folding of the hands to rest—
¹¹ and poverty will come on you like a thief
and scarcity like an armed man.

¹² A troublemaker and a villain,
who goes about with a corrupt mouth,
¹³ who winks maliciously with his eye,
signals with his feet
and motions with his fingers,
¹⁴ who plots evil with deceit in his heart—
he always stirs up conflict.

a 3 Or *Go and humble yourself,*

¹⁵ Therefore disaster will overtake him in an instant;
> he will suddenly be destroyed—without remedy.

¹⁶ There are six things the LORD hates,
> seven that are detestable to him:
¹⁷   haughty eyes,
>   a lying tongue,
>   hands that shed innocent blood,
¹⁸   a heart that devises wicked schemes,
>   feet that are quick to rush into evil,
¹⁹   a false witness who pours out lies
>   and a person who stirs up conflict in the community.

Warning Against Adultery

²⁰ My son, keep your father's command
> and do not forsake your mother's teaching.
²¹ Bind them always on your heart;
> fasten them around your neck.
²² When you walk, they will guide you;
> when you sleep, they will watch over you;
> when you awake, they will speak to you.
²³ For this command is a lamp,
> this teaching is a light,
> and correction and instruction
> are the way to life,
²⁴ keeping you from your neighbor's wife,
> from the smooth talk of a wayward woman.

²⁵ Do not lust in your heart after her beauty
> or let her captivate you with her eyes.

²⁶ For a prostitute can be had for a loaf of bread,
> but another man's wife preys on your very life.
²⁷ Can a man scoop fire into his lap
> without his clothes being burned?
²⁸ Can a man walk on hot coals
> without his feet being scorched?
²⁹ So is he who sleeps with another man's wife;
> no one who touches her will go unpunished.

³⁰ People do not despise a thief if he steals
> to satisfy his hunger when he is starving.

³¹ Yet if he is caught, he must pay sevenfold,
   though it costs him all the wealth of his house.
³² But a man who commits adultery has no sense;
   whoever does so destroys himself.
³³ Blows and disgrace are his lot,
   and his shame will never be wiped away.

³⁴ For jealousy arouses a husband's fury,
   and he will show no mercy when he takes revenge.
³⁵ He will not accept any compensation;
   he will refuse a bribe, however great it is.

REFLECTION

on PROVERBS 6:16–19

Scripture tells us that God is love (see 1 John 4:8,16), but it also tells us there are some things he hates—and it says so in a book of wisdom. That's because wisdom is much more than getting principles and instructions from God. If wisdom were simply good advice—information passed on to us impersonally—we could develop some religious practices and call it righteousness. But in God's kingdom, wisdom is much more relational. We can't really become wise outside of personal interaction with God. He doesn't just *give* wisdom; he *is* wisdom.

When we spend time with God and learn what he loves and hates, that affects our hearts. We begin to cultivate the same passions. We develop a distaste for pride, deception, violence and scheming, and we develop an affection for what he loves, including his people and his mission. When our passions align with God's, wisdom happens much more naturally than when we try to absorb principles and implement them in our lives. A heart that beats with God's inevitably generates thoughts and actions consistent with God's heart. ✤

day 7

Warning Against the Adulterous Woman

7 My son, keep my words
  and store up my commands within you.
² Keep my commands and you will live;
  guard my teachings as the apple of your eye.
³ Bind them on your fingers;
  write them on the tablet of your heart.
⁴ Say to wisdom, "You are my sister,"
  and to insight, "You are my relative."
⁵ They will keep you from the adulterous woman,
  from the wayward woman with her seductive words.

⁶ At the window of my house
  I looked down through the lattice.
⁷ I saw among the simple,
  I noticed among the young men,
  a youth who had no sense.
⁸ He was going down the street near her corner,
  walking along in the direction of her house
⁹ at twilight, as the day was fading,
  as the dark of night set in.

¹⁰ Then out came a woman to meet him,
  dressed like a prostitute and with crafty intent.
¹¹ (She is unruly and defiant,
  her feet never stay at home;
¹² now in the street, now in the squares,
  at every corner she lurks.)
¹³ She took hold of him and kissed him
  and with a brazen face she said:

¹⁴ "Today I fulfilled my vows,
  and I have food from my fellowship offering at home.
¹⁵ So I came out to meet you;
  I looked for you and have found you!

¹⁶I have covered my bed
　　with colored linens from Egypt.
¹⁷I have perfumed my bed
　　with myrrh, aloes and cinnamon.
¹⁸Come, let's drink deeply of love till morning;
　　let's enjoy ourselves with love!
¹⁹My husband is not at home;
　　he has gone on a long journey.
²⁰He took his purse filled with money
　　and will not be home till full moon."

²¹With persuasive words she led him astray;
　　she seduced him with her smooth talk.
²²All at once he followed her
　　like an ox going to the slaughter,
　like a deer[a] stepping into a noose[b]
²³　till an arrow pierces his liver,
　like a bird darting into a snare,
　　little knowing it will cost him his life.

²⁴Now then, my sons, listen to me;
　　pay attention to what I say.
²⁵Do not let your heart turn to her ways
　　or stray into her paths.
²⁶Many are the victims she has brought down;
　　her slain are a mighty throng.
²⁷Her house is a highway to the grave,
　　leading down to the chambers of death.

[a] 22 Syriac (see also Septuagint); Hebrew *fool*   [b] 22 The meaning of the Hebrew for this line is uncertain.

REFLECTION

on **PROVERBS 7:1–4**

In Deuteronomy 6:6–9, Moses told the Israelites to fully integrate the law into their lives: to talk about it at home and on the road, when they went to bed at night and when they got up in the morning, to bind it to their foreheads and hands and write it on their doorframes as constant reminders. Solomon uses similar language to impress upon his sons the importance of his advice. In fact, in many places he elevates his words from "advice" to "commands" (see Proverbs 7:1–2). These issues are that important.

True wisdom is a treasure. Like a collector who can't stop adding to a collection or a jeweler who can't stop gazing at the beauty of jewels, we are to gather and savor divine truth, marveling at its beauty and enjoying its blessings. The mind of God, to whatever extent we can share it, fills us with his presence and leads us in his ways. We are to get up close and personal with his wisdom and insight, seeing them as "relative[s]." Then God's mind becomes a part of who we are.   ✤

day 8

Wisdom's Call

8 Does not wisdom call out?
Does not understanding raise her voice?

2 At the highest point along the way,
where the paths meet, she takes her stand;

3 beside the gate leading into the city,
at the entrance, she cries aloud:

4 "To you, O people, I call out;
I raise my voice to all mankind.

5 You who are simple, gain prudence;
you who are foolish, set your hearts on it.[a]

6 Listen, for I have trustworthy things to say;
I open my lips to speak what is right.

7 My mouth speaks what is true,
for my lips detest wickedness.

8 All the words of my mouth are just;
none of them is crooked or perverse.

9 To the discerning all of them are right;
they are upright to those who have found knowledge.

10 Choose my instruction instead of silver,
knowledge rather than choice gold,

11 for wisdom is more precious than rubies,
and nothing you desire can compare with her.

12 "I, wisdom, dwell together with prudence;
I possess knowledge and discretion.

13 To fear the LORD is to hate evil;
I hate pride and arrogance,
evil behavior and perverse speech.

14 Counsel and sound judgment are mine;
I have insight, I have power.

15 By me kings reign
and rulers issue decrees that are just;

---

[a] 5 Septuagint; Hebrew *foolish, instruct your minds*

¹⁶ by me princes govern,
  and nobles—all who rule on earth.ᵃ
¹⁷ I love those who love me,
  and those who seek me find me.
¹⁸ With me are riches and honor,
  enduring wealth and prosperity.
¹⁹ My fruit is better than fine gold;
  what I yield surpasses choice silver.
²⁰ I walk in the way of righteousness,
  along the paths of justice,
²¹ bestowing a rich inheritance on those who love me
  and making their treasuries full.

²² "The Lᴏʀᴅ brought me forth as the first of his works,ᵇ,ᶜ
  before his deeds of old;
²³ I was formed long ages ago,
  at the very beginning, when the world came to be.
²⁴ When there were no watery depths, I was given birth,
  when there were no springs overflowing with water;
²⁵ before the mountains were settled in place,
  before the hills, I was given birth,
²⁶ before he made the world or its fields
  or any of the dust of the earth.
²⁷ I was there when he set the heavens in place,
  when he marked out the horizon on the face of the deep,
²⁸ when he established the clouds above
  and fixed securely the fountains of the deep,
²⁹ when he gave the sea its boundary
  so the waters would not overstep his command,
  and when he marked out the foundations of the earth.
³⁰   Then I was constantlyᵈ at his side.
  I was filled with delight day after day,
  rejoicing always in his presence,
³¹ rejoicing in his whole world
  and delighting in mankind.

³² "Now then, my children, listen to me;
  blessed are those who keep my ways.

ᵃ 16 Some Hebrew manuscripts and Septuagint; other Hebrew manuscripts
all righteous rulers   ᵇ 22 Or *way*; or *dominion*   ᶜ 22 Or *The* Lᴏʀᴅ
possessed me at the beginning of his work; or *The* Lᴏʀᴅ *brought me forth at the
beginning of his work*   ᵈ 30 Or *was the artisan*; or *was a little child*

³³ Listen to my instruction and be wise;
  do not disregard it.
³⁴ Blessed are those who listen to me,
  watching daily at my doors,
  waiting at my doorway.
³⁵ For those who find me find life
  and receive favor from the Lord.
³⁶ But those who fail to find me harm themselves;
  all who hate me love death."

REFLECTION

on **PROVERBS 8:1–4**

Wisdom calls out to us (see Proverbs 1:20–21; 8:1–4). Apparently, so does folly (see Proverbs 9:13–15). Their methods of communication are similar; they sit in public places shouting their advice to all who will listen. The difference between them is in what they say and the hearts they connect with. Those who are inclined toward God—who love him and want to do his will—will hear the voice of wisdom and respond. Those who have little depth and no desire for God—who can't see beyond themselves and the present moment—will hear the voice of folly and respond. Two voices, two kinds of hearts; as a result, two drastically different journeys.

Which voice will we choose to trust? The question is more complicated than it seems: It doesn't involve just a single choice but rather a series of choices every day, and sometimes folly imitates wisdom. But prayer, patience and a commitment to truth will reveal the difference and give us the discipline and courage to choose well. Hearts that crave wisdom will choose the right voice. ✤

day 9

Invitations of Wisdom and Folly

9 Wisdom has built her house;
  she has set up[a] its seven pillars.
2 She has prepared her meat and mixed her wine;
  she has also set her table.
3 She has sent out her servants, and she calls
  from the highest point of the city,
4 "Let all who are simple come to my house!"
To those who have no sense she says,
5 "Come, eat my food
  and drink the wine I have mixed.
6 Leave your simple ways and you will live;
  walk in the way of insight."

7 Whoever corrects a mocker invites insults;
  whoever rebukes the wicked incurs abuse.
8 Do not rebuke mockers or they will hate you;
  rebuke the wise and they will love you.
9 Instruct the wise and they will be wiser still;
  teach the righteous and they will add to their learning.

10 The fear of the Lord is the beginning of wisdom,
  and knowledge of the Holy One is understanding.
11 For through wisdom[b] your days will be many,
  and years will be added to your life.
12 If you are wise, your wisdom will reward you;
  if you are a mocker, you alone will suffer.

13 Folly is an unruly woman;
  she is simple and knows nothing.
14 She sits at the door of her house,
  on a seat at the highest point of the city,
15 calling out to those who pass by,
  who go straight on their way,

a 1 Septuagint, Syriac and Targum; Hebrew *has hewn out*
b 11 Septuagint, Syriac and Targum; Hebrew *me*

¹⁶ "Let all who are simple come to my house!"
  To those who have no sense she says,
¹⁷ "Stolen water is sweet;
    food eaten in secret is delicious!"
¹⁸ But little do they know that the dead are there,
    that her guests are deep in the realm of the dead.

REFLECTION

on **PROVERBS 9:10**

Jacob wrestled with God and was forever changed (see Genesis 32:22–32). Isaiah saw God on his throne, cried out for mercy and was cleansed and commissioned as the Lord's prophet (see Isaiah 6:1–13). John had a vision of the risen Christ and was practically paralyzed by the sight (see Revelation 1:12–18). In each of these cases, a glimpse of majesty gave them a changed and lasting perspective on their lives, their world and their God. Clearly they had some degree of wisdom before their encounter—they all had experienced God and displayed wisdom—but being overwhelmingly awed by him shaped them forever.

  That's our goal: to increasingly encounter God in such a way that we are radically changed. When we get glimpses of who he is, it changes our perspective. Our priorities shift and our attitudes bend to reflect his nature. His mission becomes much more relevant, his character becomes much more beautiful and his presence becomes more real. He becomes the basis of our lives, and wisdom flows freely from such a foundation.   ❖

day 10

Proverbs of Solomon

10 The proverbs of Solomon:

A wise son brings joy to his father,
　　but a foolish son brings grief to his mother.

[2] Ill-gotten treasures have no lasting value,
　　but righteousness delivers from death.

[3] The LORD does not let the righteous go hungry,
　　but he thwarts the craving of the wicked.

[4] Lazy hands make for poverty,
　　but diligent hands bring wealth.

[5] He who gathers crops in summer is a prudent son,
　　but he who sleeps during harvest is a disgraceful son.

[6] Blessings crown the head of the righteous,
　　but violence overwhelms the mouth of the wicked.[a]

[7] The name of the righteous is used in blessings,[b]
　　but the name of the wicked will rot.

[8] The wise in heart accept commands,
　　but a chattering fool comes to ruin.

[9] Whoever walks in integrity walks securely,
　　but whoever takes crooked paths will be found out.

[10] Whoever winks maliciously causes grief,
　　and a chattering fool comes to ruin.

[11] The mouth of the righteous is a fountain of life,
　　but the mouth of the wicked conceals violence.

[12] Hatred stirs up conflict,
　　but love covers over all wrongs.

[a] 6 Or *righteous, / but the mouth of the wicked conceals violence*
[b] 7 See Gen. 48:20.

¹³ Wisdom is found on the lips of the discerning,
 but a rod is for the back of one who has no sense.

¹⁴ The wise store up knowledge,
 but the mouth of a fool invites ruin.

¹⁵ The wealth of the rich is their fortified city,
 but poverty is the ruin of the poor.

¹⁶ The wages of the righteous is life,
 but the earnings of the wicked are sin and death.

¹⁷ Whoever heeds discipline shows the way to life,
 but whoever ignores correction leads others astray.

¹⁸ Whoever conceals hatred with lying lips
 and spreads slander is a fool.

¹⁹ Sin is not ended by multiplying words,
 but the prudent hold their tongues.

²⁰ The tongue of the righteous is choice silver,
 but the heart of the wicked is of little value.

²¹ The lips of the righteous nourish many,
 but fools die for lack of sense.

²² The blessing of the Lord brings wealth,
 without painful toil for it.

²³ A fool finds pleasure in wicked schemes,
 but a person of understanding delights in wisdom.

²⁴ What the wicked dread will overtake them;
 what the righteous desire will be granted.

²⁵ When the storm has swept by, the wicked are gone,
 but the righteous stand firm forever.

²⁶ As vinegar to the teeth and smoke to the eyes,
 so are sluggards to those who send them.

²⁷ The fear of the Lord adds length to life,
 but the years of the wicked are cut short.

²⁸ The prospect of the righteous is joy,
 but the hopes of the wicked come to nothing.

²⁹ The way of the LORD is a refuge for the blameless,
  but it is the ruin of those who do evil.

³⁰ The righteous will never be uprooted,
  but the wicked will not remain in the land.

³¹ From the mouth of the righteous comes the fruit of wisdom,
  but a perverse tongue will be silenced.

³² The lips of the righteous know what finds favor,
  but the mouth of the wicked only what is perverse.

REFLECTION

on **PROVERBS 10:24**

This proverb reminds us that our expectations may shape our lives more than we realize. Those who worry constantly about the details of life never run out of things to worry about—and often find their worries were valid. Those who believe God answers prayer often experience answers. Those who expect to see God's goodness usually do.

God honors the inclinations of our hearts. He prefers to shape them himself, but when we draw close to him, he plants many of his desires within us. When people insist on keeping him at arm's length, he honors their wishes as well.

Perhaps that's one reason why we are urged, in Proverbs 4:23, to guard our hearts. We need to be intentional about the images, moods and expectations we hold within us. Much of what we receive from God is realized on the basis of our faith. If we don't have any faith, what we dread may be worth dreading. But if we do have faith, often our desires will be granted. ♣

day11

11 The Lord detests dishonest scales,
   but accurate weights find favor with him.

² When pride comes, then comes disgrace,
   but with humility comes wisdom.

³ The integrity of the upright guides them,
   but the unfaithful are destroyed by their duplicity.

⁴ Wealth is worthless in the day of wrath,
   but righteousness delivers from death.

⁵ The righteousness of the blameless makes their paths straight,
   but the wicked are brought down by their own wickedness.

⁶ The righteousness of the upright delivers them,
   but the unfaithful are trapped by evil desires.

⁷ Hopes placed in mortals die with them;
   all the promise of*ᵃ* their power comes to nothing.

⁸ The righteous person is rescued from trouble,
   and it falls on the wicked instead.

⁹ With their mouths the godless destroy their neighbors,
   but through knowledge the righteous escape.

¹⁰ When the righteous prosper, the city rejoices;
   when the wicked perish, there are shouts of joy.

¹¹ Through the blessing of the upright a city is exalted,
   but by the mouth of the wicked it is destroyed.

¹² Whoever derides their neighbor has no sense,
   but the one who has understanding holds their tongue.

¹³ A gossip betrays a confidence,
   but a trustworthy person keeps a secret.

---

*ᵃ 7 Two Hebrew manuscripts; most Hebrew manuscripts, Vulgate, Syriac
and Targum When the wicked die, their hope perishes; / all they expected from*

14 For lack of guidance a nation falls,
    but victory is won through many advisers.

15 Whoever puts up security for a stranger will surely suffer,
    but whoever refuses to shake hands in pledge is safe.

16 A kindhearted woman gains honor,
    but ruthless men gain only wealth.

17 Those who are kind benefit themselves,
    but the cruel bring ruin on themselves.

18 A wicked person earns deceptive wages,
    but the one who sows righteousness reaps a sure reward.

19 Truly the righteous attain life,
    but whoever pursues evil finds death.

20 The Lord detests those whose hearts are perverse,
    but he delights in those whose ways are blameless.

21 Be sure of this: The wicked will not go unpunished,
    but those who are righteous will go free.

22 Like a gold ring in a pig's snout
    is a beautiful woman who shows no discretion.

23 The desire of the righteous ends only in good,
    but the hope of the wicked only in wrath.

24 One person gives freely, yet gains even more;
    another withholds unduly, but comes to poverty.

25 A generous person will prosper;
    whoever refreshes others will be refreshed.

26 People curse the one who hoards grain,
    but they pray God's blessing on the one who is willing to
        sell.

27 Whoever seeks good finds favor,
    but evil comes to one who searches for it.

28 Those who trust in their riches will fall,
    but the righteous will thrive like a green leaf.

29 Whoever brings ruin on their family will inherit only wind,
    and the fool will be servant to the wise.

³⁰ The fruit of the righteous is a tree of life,
   and the one who is wise saves lives.

³¹ If the righteous receive their due on earth,
   how much more the ungodly and the sinner!

REFLECTION

on **PROVERBS 11:2**

Pride versus humility is a consistent theme not only in Proverbs but throughout Scripture. God detests the proud, we are told (see Proverbs 16:5). He opposes them, but shows favor to the humble (see Proverbs 3:34). Pride brings people down, but the humble are eventually lifted up (see 1 Peter 5:5–6). Again and again we see this dynamic not only in the Bible but also in our own lives and in the people around us.

Why is God so opposed to pride? For one thing, it's delusional. When we know who God is and who we are in comparison, we can't help but be humble. Any other perspective is a false view of reality. But more than that, pride seems to be the source of all other sins. It has satanic implications (see Isaiah 14:12–14; Ezekiel 28:12–17). When people begin to elevate themselves above others, dishonesty, contempt, manipulation and a host of other offenses suddenly become justifiable. Pride corrupts wisdom, while humility attracts it. Throughout Proverbs, pride and folly go hand in hand. Only the humble can be wise.   ❖

day 12

12 Whoever loves discipline loves knowledge,
but whoever hates correction is stupid.

2 Good people obtain favor from the LORD,
but he condemns those who devise wicked schemes.

3 No one can be established through wickedness,
but the righteous cannot be uprooted.

4 A wife of noble character is her husband's crown,
but a disgraceful wife is like decay in his bones.

5 The plans of the righteous are just,
but the advice of the wicked is deceitful.

6 The words of the wicked lie in wait for blood,
but the speech of the upright rescues them.

7 The wicked are overthrown and are no more,
but the house of the righteous stands firm.

8 A person is praised according to their prudence,
and one with a warped mind is despised.

9 Better to be a nobody and yet have a servant
than pretend to be somebody and have no food.

10 The righteous care for the needs of their animals,
but the kindest acts of the wicked are cruel.

11 Those who work their land will have abundant food,
but those who chase fantasies have no sense.

12 The wicked desire the stronghold of evildoers,
but the root of the righteous endures.

13 Evildoers are trapped by their sinful talk,
and so the innocent escape trouble.

14 From the fruit of their lips people are filled with good things,
and the work of their hands brings them reward.

¹⁵ The way of fools seems right to them,
 but the wise listen to advice.

¹⁶ Fools show their annoyance at once,
 but the prudent overlook an insult.

¹⁷ An honest witness tells the truth,
 but a false witness tells lies.

¹⁸ The words of the reckless pierce like swords,
 but the tongue of the wise brings healing.

¹⁹ Truthful lips endure forever,
 but a lying tongue lasts only a moment.

²⁰ Deceit is in the hearts of those who plot evil,
 but those who promote peace have joy.

²¹ No harm overtakes the righteous,
 but the wicked have their fill of trouble.

²² The Lᴏʀᴅ detests lying lips,
 but he delights in people who are trustworthy.

²³ The prudent keep their knowledge to themselves,
 but a fool's heart blurts out folly.

²⁴ Diligent hands will rule,
 but laziness ends in forced labor.

²⁵ Anxiety weighs down the heart,
 but a kind word cheers it up.

²⁶ The righteous choose their friends carefully,
 but the way of the wicked leads them astray.

²⁷ The lazy do not roast[a] any game,
 but the diligent feed on the riches of the hunt.

²⁸ In the way of righteousness there is life;
 along that path is immortality.

[a] 27 The meaning of the Hebrew for this word is uncertain.

REFLECTION

on **PROVERBS 12:17–19**

The difference between wisdom and folly is perhaps nowhere clearer than in our speech. Proverbs 12 repeatedly contrasts the foolish and the wise in terms of what comes out of their mouths. The words of the wicked are treacherous, while the words of the upright bring safety (verse 6). Sinful talk becomes a trap, but the innocent become free (verse 13). Proper speech can bring us good things (verse 14). Truth or lies (verse 17), wounds or healing (verse 18), momentary or lasting (verse 19), God's disdain or God's delight (verse 22)—there is a lot at stake in what flows out of our hearts and off of our tongues.

We know this to be true. All of us have made foolish comments we regretted. The solution isn't simply to discipline our words—although that's a great start—but to be transformed from within. Pure fountains don't spew dirty water. Our words are symptoms of an internal condition. If the symptoms alarm us, we know what to do: Cultivate wisdom in our innermost being by drawing nearer and nearer to God.   ✣

day 13

13 A wise son heeds his father's instruction,
but a mocker does not respond to rebukes.

2 From the fruit of their lips people enjoy good things,
but the unfaithful have an appetite for violence.

3 Those who guard their lips preserve their lives,
but those who speak rashly will come to ruin.

4 A sluggard's appetite is never filled,
but the desires of the diligent are fully satisfied.

5 The righteous hate what is false,
but the wicked make themselves a stench
and bring shame on themselves.

6 Righteousness guards the person of integrity,
but wickedness overthrows the sinner.

7 One person pretends to be rich, yet has nothing;
another pretends to be poor, yet has great wealth.

8 A person's riches may ransom their life,
but the poor cannot respond to threatening rebukes.

9 The light of the righteous shines brightly,
but the lamp of the wicked is snuffed out.

10 Where there is strife, there is pride,
but wisdom is found in those who take advice.

11 Dishonest money dwindles away,
but whoever gathers money little by little makes it grow.

12 Hope deferred makes the heart sick,
but a longing fulfilled is a tree of life.

13 Whoever scorns instruction will pay for it,
but whoever respects a command is rewarded.

14 The teaching of the wise is a fountain of life,
turning a person from the snares of death.

¹⁵ Good judgment wins favor,
 but the way of the unfaithful leads to their destruction.^{*a*}

¹⁶ All who are prudent act with^{*b*} knowledge,
 but fools expose their folly.

¹⁷ A wicked messenger falls into trouble,
 but a trustworthy envoy brings healing.

¹⁸ Whoever disregards discipline comes to poverty and shame,
 but whoever heeds correction is honored.

¹⁹ A longing fulfilled is sweet to the soul,
 but fools detest turning from evil.

²⁰ Walk with the wise and become wise,
 for a companion of fools suffers harm.

²¹ Trouble pursues the sinner,
 but the righteous are rewarded with good things.

²² A good person leaves an inheritance for their children's
  children,
 but a sinner's wealth is stored up for the righteous.

²³ An unplowed field produces food for the poor,
 but injustice sweeps it away.

²⁴ Whoever spares the rod hates their children,
 but the one who loves their children is careful to discipline
  them.

²⁵ The righteous eat to their hearts' content,
 but the stomach of the wicked goes hungry.

---

a 15 Septuagint and Syriac; the meaning of the Hebrew for this phrase is uncertain. *b* 16 Or *prudent protect themselves through*

REFLECTION

on PROVERBS 13:12

We all yearn for something. We have strong desires that we bring to God, hoping he will fulfill them. Sometimes we're afraid to get our hopes up—we've often heard that God will give us what we need but not necessarily what we want—yet, as the poet Alexander Pope said, hope springs eternal in the human breast. Something in us refuses to give up.

God is well acquainted with our longings; Scripture is filled with expressions of them. And the glimpses of "longing fulfilled" — Abraham and Sarah finally getting the last "laugh" with the birth of Isaac (see Genesis 21:1 – 7), Israel's song of celebration on the safe side of the Red Sea in Exodus 15, Hannah's prayer of gratitude (see 1 Samuel 2:1 – 10), the exhilaration of the exiles in Psalm 126 — stir our hopes even more. Our "hope deferred" reminds us that God's greatest works often involve painful years of waiting. But the "tree of life" — an image seen only in the Garden of Eden (see Genesis 2:9), the new Jerusalem (see Revelation 22:2) and here in Proverbs (see also 3:18; 11:30; 15:4) — gives us hope that our longings will be fulfilled in God's time.   ❖

day14

14 The wise woman builds her house,
but with her own hands the foolish one tears hers down.

²Whoever fears the Lᴏʀᴅ walks uprightly,
but those who despise him are devious in their ways.

³A fool's mouth lashes out with pride,
but the lips of the wise protect them.

⁴Where there are no oxen, the manger is empty,
but from the strength of an ox come abundant harvests.

⁵An honest witness does not deceive,
but a false witness pours out lies.

⁶The mocker seeks wisdom and finds none,
but knowledge comes easily to the discerning.

⁷Stay away from a fool,
for you will not find knowledge on their lips.

⁸The wisdom of the prudent is to give thought to their ways,
but the folly of fools is deception.

⁹Fools mock at making amends for sin,
but goodwill is found among the upright.

¹⁰Each heart knows its own bitterness,
and no one else can share its joy.

¹¹The house of the wicked will be destroyed,
but the tent of the upright will flourish.

¹²There is a way that appears to be right,
but in the end it leads to death.

¹³Even in laughter the heart may ache,
and rejoicing may end in grief.

¹⁴The faithless will be fully repaid for their ways,
and the good rewarded for theirs.

¹⁵The simple believe anything,
  but the prudent give thought to their steps.

¹⁶The wise fear the Lord and shun evil,
  but a fool is hotheaded and yet feels secure.

¹⁷A quick-tempered person does foolish things,
  and the one who devises evil schemes is hated.

¹⁸The simple inherit folly,
  but the prudent are crowned with knowledge.

¹⁹Evildoers will bow down in the presence of the good,
  and the wicked at the gates of the righteous.

²⁰The poor are shunned even by their neighbors,
  but the rich have many friends.

²¹It is a sin to despise one's neighbor,
  but blessed is the one who is kind to the needy.

²²Do not those who plot evil go astray?
  But those who plan what is good find*a* love and faithfulness.

²³All hard work brings a profit,
  but mere talk leads only to poverty.

²⁴The wealth of the wise is their crown,
  but the folly of fools yields folly.

²⁵A truthful witness saves lives,
  but a false witness is deceitful.

²⁶Whoever fears the Lord has a secure fortress,
  and for their children it will be a refuge.

²⁷The fear of the Lord is a fountain of life,
  turning a person from the snares of death.

²⁸A large population is a king's glory,
  but without subjects a prince is ruined.

²⁹Whoever is patient has great understanding,
  but one who is quick-tempered displays folly.

³⁰A heart at peace gives life to the body,
  but envy rots the bones.

a 22 Or *show*

31 Whoever oppresses the poor shows contempt for their Maker,
   but whoever is kind to the needy honors God.

32 When calamity comes, the wicked are brought down,
   but even in death the righteous seek refuge in God.

33 Wisdom reposes in the heart of the discerning
   and even among fools she lets herself be known. [a]

34 Righteousness exalts a nation,
   but sin condemns any people.

35 A king delights in a wise servant,
   but a shameful servant arouses his fury.

[a] 33 Hebrew; Septuagint and Syriac *discerning / but in the heart of fools she is not known*

REFLECTION

on PROVERBS 14:2

The world is full of manipulators. Some are outright deceivers trying to con anyone they can and take advantage of the innocent. Most, however, are people who are just trying to get by. They don't mean to manipulate; it's just a survival skill they have learned over the years. They have felt hurt or betrayed, so they don't trust God or others. And if God can't be trusted to provide or protect, they will just have to look out for themselves. If they don't manipulate the people around them to their own advantage, they think they will never have any advantage at all.

People who know God and trust him don't have to scheme. We don't have to drop hints, pull strings, eavesdrop for inside information, plant ideas or rearrange schedules for personal gain. We can rest in the fact that the sovereign God will work out his purposes in our lives even if we aren't on top of every detail. Trusting in his goodness gives us rest in our hearts.   ❖

day 15

15 A gentle answer turns away wrath,
but a harsh word stirs up anger.

²The tongue of the wise adorns knowledge,
but the mouth of the fool gushes folly.

³The eyes of the Lord are everywhere,
keeping watch on the wicked and the good.

⁴The soothing tongue is a tree of life,
but a perverse tongue crushes the spirit.

⁵A fool spurns a parent's discipline,
but whoever heeds correction shows prudence.

⁶The house of the righteous contains great treasure,
but the income of the wicked brings ruin.

⁷The lips of the wise spread knowledge,
but the hearts of fools are not upright.

⁸The Lord detests the sacrifice of the wicked,
but the prayer of the upright pleases him.

⁹The Lord detests the way of the wicked,
but he loves those who pursue righteousness.

¹⁰Stern discipline awaits anyone who leaves the path;
the one who hates correction will die.

¹¹Death and Destruction*a* lie open before the Lord—
how much more do human hearts!

¹²Mockers resent correction,
so they avoid the wise.

¹³A happy heart makes the face cheerful,
but heartache crushes the spirit.

a 11 Hebrew *Abaddon*

¹⁴The discerning heart seeks knowledge,
    but the mouth of a fool feeds on folly.

¹⁵All the days of the oppressed are wretched,
    but the cheerful heart has a continual feast.

¹⁶Better a little with the fear of the LORD
    than great wealth with turmoil.

¹⁷Better a small serving of vegetables with love
    than a fattened calf with hatred.

¹⁸A hot-tempered person stirs up conflict,
    but the one who is patient calms a quarrel.

¹⁹The way of the sluggard is blocked with thorns,
    but the path of the upright is a highway.

²⁰A wise son brings joy to his father,
    but a foolish man despises his mother.

²¹Folly brings joy to one who has no sense,
    but whoever has understanding keeps a straight course.

²²Plans fail for lack of counsel,
    but with many advisers they succeed.

²³A person finds joy in giving an apt reply—
    and how good is a timely word!

²⁴The path of life leads upward for the prudent
    to keep them from going down to the realm of the dead.

²⁵The LORD tears down the house of the proud,
    but he sets the widow's boundary stones in place.

²⁶The LORD detests the thoughts of the wicked,
    but gracious words are pure in his sight.

²⁷The greedy bring ruin to their households,
    but the one who hates bribes will live.

²⁸The heart of the righteous weighs its answers,
    but the mouth of the wicked gushes evil.

²⁹The LORD is far from the wicked,
    but he hears the prayer of the righteous.

³⁰ Light in a messenger's eyes brings joy to the heart,
    and good news gives health to the bones.

³¹ Whoever heeds life-giving correction
    will be at home among the wise.

³² Those who disregard discipline despise themselves,
    but the one who heeds correction gains understanding.

³³ Wisdom's instruction is to fear the LORD,
    and humility comes before honor.

REFLECTION

on **PROVERBS 15:1–2,4**

We are told elsewhere in Proverbs that wise words bring healing (see 12:18) and that the tongue contains "the power of life and death" (Proverbs 18:21). Here we see that a gentle answer defuses anger, wise words enhance knowledge and soothing words bring life. That's a lot of power for a small part of the body, but the rest of Scripture and our own experience affirm the impact of words. We can wreak a lot of havoc with what we say—James compares our tongues to a spark that can start a forest fire (see James 3:5–6). But the opposite is also true: We can praise God and bless others with positive, encouraging, praiseworthy statements of truth.

Think of that. We can make a dramatic difference in people's lives simply by asking God to minister to them, speaking a blessing over them, affirming their gifts, encouraging them about their God-given potential and more. We can heal past wounds, offer forgiveness and declare God's love. Why would we be reluctant to wield that kind of power? Words of affirmation, blessing and encouragement cost us nothing, but they can accomplish great things.   ❖

day16

16 To humans belong the plans of the heart,
but from the LORD comes the proper answer of the tongue.

2 All a person's ways seem pure to them,
but motives are weighed by the LORD.

3 Commit to the LORD whatever you do,
and he will establish your plans.

4 The LORD works out everything to its proper end—
even the wicked for a day of disaster.

5 The LORD detests all the proud of heart.
Be sure of this: They will not go unpunished.

6 Through love and faithfulness sin is atoned for;
through the fear of the LORD evil is avoided.

7 When the LORD takes pleasure in anyone's way,
he causes their enemies to make peace with them.

8 Better a little with righteousness
than much gain with injustice.

9 In their hearts humans plan their course,
but the LORD establishes their steps.

10 The lips of a king speak as an oracle,
and his mouth does not betray justice.

11 Honest scales and balances belong to the LORD;
all the weights in the bag are of his making.

12 Kings detest wrongdoing,
for a throne is established through righteousness.

13 Kings take pleasure in honest lips;
they value the one who speaks what is right.

14 A king's wrath is a messenger of death,
but the wise will appease it.

¹⁵ When a king's face brightens, it means life;
     his favor is like a rain cloud in spring.

¹⁶ How much better to get wisdom than gold,
     to get insight rather than silver!

¹⁷ The highway of the upright avoids evil;
     those who guard their ways preserve their lives.

¹⁸ Pride goes before destruction,
     a haughty spirit before a fall.

¹⁹ Better to be lowly in spirit along with the oppressed
     than to share plunder with the proud.

²⁰ Whoever gives heed to instruction prospers,ᵃ
     and blessed is the one who trusts in the LORD.

²¹ The wise in heart are called discerning,
     and gracious words promote instruction.ᵇ

²² Prudence is a fountain of life to the prudent,
     but folly brings punishment to fools.

²³ The hearts of the wise make their mouths prudent,
     and their lips promote instruction.ᶜ

²⁴ Gracious words are a honeycomb,
     sweet to the soul and healing to the bones.

²⁵ There is a way that appears to be right,
     but in the end it leads to death.

²⁶ The appetite of laborers works for them;
     their hunger drives them on.

²⁷ A scoundrel plots evil,
     and on their lips it is like a scorching fire.

²⁸ A perverse person stirs up conflict,
     and a gossip separates close friends.

²⁹ A violent person entices their neighbor
     and leads them down a path that is not good.

ᵃ 20 Or *whoever speaks prudently finds what is good*   ᵇ 21 Or *words make a person persuasive*   ᶜ 23 Or *prudent / and make their lips persuasive*

³⁰Whoever winks with their eye is plotting perversity;
    whoever purses their lips is bent on evil.

³¹Gray hair is a crown of splendor;
    it is attained in the way of righteousness.

³²Better a patient person than a warrior,
    one with self-control than one who takes a city.

³³The lot is cast into the lap,
    but its every decision is from the LORD.

REFLECTION

on PROVERBS 16:7

It sounds like an astounding promise: If God takes pleasure, or is pleased, with us, he causes our enemies to make peace with us. We do see examples from the Bible of this principle when we look at the reigns of godly Asa and Jehoshaphat (see 2 Chronicles 14:2,6–7; 17:3–6,10). But we run into a problem when we realize that God was pleased with Jesus, yet his enemies hated him and executed him. God was pleased with Joseph, Moses, David, the prophets, the disciples, Paul and many more, yet all faced fierce opposition. So what is this proverb saying?

The general principle here is that a life that pleases God will be above reproach, and the person will find favor with others. But we need to remember that, like many proverbs, this one doesn't apply to all circumstances. It may be evident in a season of our lives when we desperately need God's help. Ultimately it applies to all of us, as one day no enemy will be able to touch us. For now, we are guaranteed resistance and even persecution (2 Timothy 3:12). But in the eternal scheme of things, any opposition we face is limited. The time of dealing with enemies will come to an end. That's a promise.   ❧

day17

17 Better a dry crust with peace and quiet
than a house full of feasting, with strife.

² A prudent servant will rule over a disgraceful son
and will share the inheritance as one of the family.

³ The crucible for silver and the furnace for gold,
but the LORD tests the heart.

⁴ A wicked person listens to deceitful lips;
a liar pays attention to a destructive tongue.

⁵ Whoever mocks the poor shows contempt for their Maker;
whoever gloats over disaster will not go unpunished.

⁶ Children's children are a crown to the aged,
and parents are the pride of their children.

⁷ Eloquent lips are unsuited to a godless fool—
how much worse lying lips to a ruler!

⁸ A bribe is seen as a charm by the one who gives it;
they think success will come at every turn.

⁹ Whoever would foster love covers over an offense,
but whoever repeats the matter separates close friends.

¹⁰ A rebuke impresses a discerning person
more than a hundred lashes a fool.

¹¹ Evildoers foster rebellion against God;
the messenger of death will be sent against them.

¹² Better to meet a bear robbed of her cubs
than a fool bent on folly.

¹³ Evil will never leave the house
of one who pays back evil for good.

¹⁴ Starting a quarrel is like breaching a dam;
   so drop the matter before a dispute breaks out.

¹⁵ Acquitting the guilty and condemning the innocent—
   the LORD detests them both.

¹⁶ Why should fools have money in hand to buy wisdom,
   when they are not able to understand it?

¹⁷ A friend loves at all times,
   and a brother is born for a time of adversity.

¹⁸ One who has no sense shakes hands in pledge
   and puts up security for a neighbor.

¹⁹ Whoever loves a quarrel loves sin;
   whoever builds a high gate invites destruction.

²⁰ One whose heart is corrupt does not prosper;
   one whose tongue is perverse falls into trouble.

²¹ To have a fool for a child brings grief;
   there is no joy for the parent of a godless fool.

²² A cheerful heart is good medicine,
   but a crushed spirit dries up the bones.

²³ The wicked accept bribes in secret
   to pervert the course of justice.

²⁴ A discerning person keeps wisdom in view,
   but a fool's eyes wander to the ends of the earth.

²⁵ A foolish son brings grief to his father
   and bitterness to the mother who bore him.

²⁶ If imposing a fine on the innocent is not good,
   surely to flog honest officials is not right.

²⁷ The one who has knowledge uses words with restraint,
   and whoever has understanding is even-tempered.

²⁸ Even fools are thought wise if they keep silent,
   and discerning if they hold their tongues.

REFLECTION

on **PROVERBS 17:17**

Friendship—the kind that forms into a lasting bond that can endure adversity—is a gift from God. Sometimes it seems like a rare gift; human hearts can be fickle and superficial. But out of all our acquaintances, usually one, two or maybe even several turn out to be faithful friends who will stick with us through whatever we face and who can rely on us to do the same for them. That's a privilege and a blessing from heaven.

Abraham is described in the Bible as God's "friend" (2 Chronicles 20:7; Isaiah 41:8; James 2:23), and Jesus told his disciples they weren't his servants, but his friends (see John 15:15). Friendship is important in our human relationships, but it also is what God wants from us. Yes, he is our Shepherd, our Master, our Lord ... but also our Father, Bridegroom and Friend. The relationship is meant to be deeply personal and to go both ways. Like a good friend, he "loves at all times" and sticks with us in "a time of adversity" (Proverbs 17:17). ✤

day 18

18 An unfriendly person pursues selfish ends
and against all sound judgment starts quarrels.

² Fools find no pleasure in understanding
but delight in airing their own opinions.

³ When wickedness comes, so does contempt,
and with shame comes reproach.

⁴ The words of the mouth are deep waters,
but the fountain of wisdom is a rushing stream.

⁵ It is not good to be partial to the wicked
and so deprive the innocent of justice.

⁶ The lips of fools bring them strife,
and their mouths invite a beating.

⁷ The mouths of fools are their undoing,
and their lips are a snare to their very lives.

⁸ The words of a gossip are like choice morsels;
they go down to the inmost parts.

⁹ One who is slack in his work
is brother to one who destroys.

¹⁰ The name of the Lord is a fortified tower;
the righteous run to it and are safe.

¹¹ The wealth of the rich is their fortified city;
they imagine it a wall too high to scale.

¹² Before a downfall the heart is haughty,
but humility comes before honor.

¹³ To answer before listening—
that is folly and shame.

¹⁴ The human spirit can endure in sickness,
but a crushed spirit who can bear?

¹⁵ The heart of the discerning acquires knowledge,
for the ears of the wise seek it out.

¹⁶ A gift opens the way
    and ushers the giver into the presence of the great.

¹⁷ In a lawsuit the first to speak seems right,
    until someone comes forward and cross-examines.

¹⁸ Casting the lot settles disputes
    and keeps strong opponents apart.

¹⁹ A brother wronged is more unyielding than a fortified city;
    disputes are like the barred gates of a citadel.

²⁰ From the fruit of their mouth a person's stomach is filled;
    with the harvest of their lips they are satisfied.

²¹ The tongue has the power of life and death,
    and those who love it will eat its fruit.

²² He who finds a wife finds what is good
    and receives favor from the LORD.

²³ The poor plead for mercy,
    but the rich answer harshly.

²⁴ One who has unreliable friends soon comes to ruin,
    but there is a friend who sticks closer than a brother.

REFLECTION

on PROVERBS 18:5

God loves justice. In fact, justice and righteousness are the "founda-tion" of his throne (Psalm 89:14; 97:2). We know him as a God of mercy. He graciously withholds judgment from those who believe in him and accept his Son's sacrifice on their behalf. But justice—compassion for the poor, weak, oppressed and brokenhearted—is as prominent a theme in Scripture as evangelism and prayer. It's part of who God is.

The Bible never insists that we be vigilant about defending our rights. Jesus was quite clear about that in the Sermon on the Mount. But the Bible certainly urges us to be vigilant about protecting the rights of others, especially those who are at a social disadvantage. Depriving the innocent, the weak or the disadvantaged of justice is a sin in God's eyes, as numerous psalms and passages from the prophets testify (see, for example, Psalm 11:4–7; 12:5; Isaiah 3:13–15; Ezekiel 22:24–31; Micah 2:1–11). When we love justice, we are being like God himself.   ✤

day 19

19 Better the poor whose walk is blameless
than a fool whose lips are perverse.

²Desire without knowledge is not good—
how much more will hasty feet miss the way!

³A person's own folly leads to their ruin,
yet their heart rages against the Lord.

⁴Wealth attracts many friends,
but even the closest friend of the poor person deserts them.

⁵A false witness will not go unpunished,
and whoever pours out lies will not go free.

⁶Many curry favor with a ruler,
and everyone is the friend of one who gives gifts.

⁷The poor are shunned by all their relatives—
how much more do their friends avoid them!
Though the poor pursue them with pleading,
they are nowhere to be found.ᵃ

⁸The one who gets wisdom loves life;
the one who cherishes understanding will soon prosper.

⁹A false witness will not go unpunished,
and whoever pours out lies will perish.

¹⁰It is not fitting for a fool to live in luxury—
how much worse for a slave to rule over princes!

¹¹A person's wisdom yields patience;
it is to one's glory to overlook an offense.

¹²A king's rage is like the roar of a lion,
but his favor is like dew on the grass.

ᵃ 7 The meaning of the Hebrew for this sentence is uncertain.

¹³ A foolish child is a father's ruin,
and a quarrelsome wife is like
the constant dripping of a leaky roof.

¹⁴ Houses and wealth are inherited from parents,
but a prudent wife is from the LORD.

¹⁵ Laziness brings on deep sleep,
and the shiftless go hungry.

¹⁶ Whoever keeps commandments keeps their life,
but whoever shows contempt for their ways will die.

¹⁷ Whoever is kind to the poor lends to the LORD,
and he will reward them for what they have done.

¹⁸ Discipline your children, for in that there is hope;
do not be a willing party to their death.

¹⁹ A hot-tempered person must pay the penalty;
rescue them, and you will have to do it again.

²⁰ Listen to advice and accept discipline,
and at the end you will be counted among the wise.

²¹ Many are the plans in a person's heart,
but it is the LORD's purpose that prevails.

²² What a person desires is unfailing love[a];
better to be poor than a liar.

²³ The fear of the LORD leads to life;
then one rests content, untouched by trouble.

²⁴ A sluggard buries his hand in the dish;
he will not even bring it back to his mouth!

²⁵ Flog a mocker, and the simple will learn prudence;
rebuke the discerning, and they will gain knowledge.

²⁶ Whoever robs their father and drives out their mother
is a child who brings shame and disgrace.

²⁷ Stop listening to instruction, my son,
and you will stray from the words of knowledge.

[a] 22 Or *Greed is a person's shame*

[28] A corrupt witness mocks at justice,
>   and the mouth of the wicked gulps down evil.

[29] Penalties are prepared for mockers,
>   and beatings for the backs of fools.

REFLECTION

on **PROVERBS 19:3**

We hardly notice we're doing it, although some of us do it often. We get mad at God for whatever hardship we find ourselves in. Yet when we dig down to the root of the hardship, we often find that we brought it on ourselves, either by an unwise decision or by unwisely avoiding a decision that could have prevented it. The finger we point at God could easily be turned back toward us.

Not all hardship is our own fault. We face many trials that we did not cause. In any hardship, we should not embrace the attitude of many guilt-ridden individuals who, whenever something bad happens, assume they did something to deserve it. But we also shouldn't be like the fools who rage at God for the ruin that resulted from their own folly. We have to own up to our decisions (and our indecisions), learn from them, ask God to teach us better ways and move forward in his grace. It's called personal responsibility. And it produces wisdom. ✤

day20

20 Wine is a mocker and beer a brawler;
whoever is led astray by them is not wise.

²A king's wrath strikes terror like the roar of a lion;
those who anger him forfeit their lives.

³It is to one's honor to avoid strife,
but every fool is quick to quarrel.

⁴Sluggards do not plow in season;
so at harvest time they look but find nothing.

⁵The purposes of a person's heart are deep waters,
but one who has insight draws them out.

⁶Many claim to have unfailing love,
but a faithful person who can find?

⁷The righteous lead blameless lives;
blessed are their children after them.

⁸When a king sits on his throne to judge,
he winnows out all evil with his eyes.

⁹Who can say, "I have kept my heart pure;
I am clean and without sin"?

¹⁰Differing weights and differing measures—
the Lᴏʀᴅ detests them both.

¹¹Even small children are known by their actions,
so is their conduct really pure and upright?

¹²Ears that hear and eyes that see—
the Lᴏʀᴅ has made them both.

¹³Do not love sleep or you will grow poor;
stay awake and you will have food to spare.

¹⁴"It's no good, it's no good!" says the buyer—
then goes off and boasts about the purchase.

¹⁵ Gold there is, and rubies in abundance,
　　but lips that speak knowledge are a rare jewel.

¹⁶ Take the garment of one who puts up security for a stranger;
　　hold it in pledge if it is done for an outsider.

¹⁷ Food gained by fraud tastes sweet,
　　but one ends up with a mouth full of gravel.

¹⁸ Plans are established by seeking advice;
　　so if you wage war, obtain guidance.

¹⁹ A gossip betrays a confidence;
　　so avoid anyone who talks too much.

²⁰ If someone curses their father or mother,
　　their lamp will be snuffed out in pitch darkness.

²¹ An inheritance claimed too soon
　　will not be blessed at the end.

²² Do not say, "I'll pay you back for this wrong!"
　　Wait for the LORD, and he will avenge you.

²³ The LORD detests differing weights,
　　and dishonest scales do not please him.

²⁴ A person's steps are directed by the LORD.
　　How then can anyone understand their own way?

²⁵ It is a trap to dedicate something rashly
　　and only later to consider one's vows.

²⁶ A wise king winnows out the wicked;
　　he drives the threshing wheel over them.

²⁷ The human spirit is[a] the lamp of the LORD
　　that sheds light on one's inmost being.

²⁸ Love and faithfulness keep a king safe;
　　through love his throne is made secure.

²⁹ The glory of young men is their strength,
　　gray hair the splendor of the old.

³⁰ Blows and wounds scrub away evil,
　　and beatings purge the inmost being.

[a] 27 Or *A person's words are*

REFLECTION

on **PROVERBS 20:10,23**

Those who try to gain a competitive advantage through dishonest means, no matter how slight, are making a powerful statement about what they believe. They are making it clear that they don't trust God to provide for them, defend them or show them his favor. Yet an alarming number of Christians are careless with their integrity. When our work ethics allow for inaccurate timesheets, hidden costs, unreliable quotes, questionable expense reports and other dubious practices, we are defrauding someone. We are being dishonest.

Few employers expect their employees to be hyper-conscientious about every minute or cent — that can become cumbersome, counterproductive and even annoying — but when an employer or client expects one thing and we give them something less, that's an ethical problem. God is a God of integrity. His people are to be known for it too.   ✤

day21

21 In the LORD's hand the king's heart is a stream of water
that he channels toward all who please him.

^{2} A person may think their own ways are right,
but the LORD weighs the heart.

^{3} To do what is right and just
is more acceptable to the LORD than sacrifice.

^{4} Haughty eyes and a proud heart—
the unplowed field of the wicked—produce sin.

^{5} The plans of the diligent lead to profit
as surely as haste leads to poverty.

^{6} A fortune made by a lying tongue
is a fleeting vapor and a deadly snare.[a]

^{7} The violence of the wicked will drag them away,
for they refuse to do what is right.

^{8} The way of the guilty is devious,
but the conduct of the innocent is upright.

^{9} Better to live on a corner of the roof
than share a house with a quarrelsome wife.

^{10} The wicked crave evil;
their neighbors get no mercy from them.

^{11} When a mocker is punished, the simple gain wisdom;
by paying attention to the wise they get knowledge.

^{12} The Righteous One[b] takes note of the house of the wicked
and brings the wicked to ruin.

^{13} Whoever shuts their ears to the cry of the poor
will also cry out and not be answered.

[a] 6 Some Hebrew manuscripts, Septuagint and Vulgate; most Hebrew
manuscripts *vapor for those who seek death*   [b] 12 Or *The righteous person*

¹⁴A gift given in secret soothes anger,
    and a bribe concealed in the cloak pacifies great wrath.

¹⁵When justice is done, it brings joy to the righteous
    but terror to evildoers.

¹⁶Whoever strays from the path of prudence
    comes to rest in the company of the dead.

¹⁷Whoever loves pleasure will become poor;
    whoever loves wine and olive oil will never be rich.

¹⁸The wicked become a ransom for the righteous,
    and the unfaithful for the upright.

¹⁹Better to live in a desert
    than with a quarrelsome and nagging wife.

²⁰The wise store up choice food and olive oil,
    but fools gulp theirs down.

²¹Whoever pursues righteousness and love
    finds life, prosperity*ᵃ* and honor.

²²One who is wise can go up against the city of the mighty
    and pull down the stronghold in which they trust.

²³Those who guard their mouths and their tongues
    keep themselves from calamity.

²⁴The proud and arrogant person—"Mocker" is his name—
    behaves with insolent fury.

²⁵The craving of a sluggard will be the death of him,
    because his hands refuse to work.
²⁶All day long he craves for more,
    but the righteous give without sparing.

²⁷The sacrifice of the wicked is detestable—
    how much more so when brought with evil intent!

²⁸A false witness will perish,
    but a careful listener will testify successfully.

²⁹The wicked put up a bold front,
    but the upright give thought to their ways.

ᵃ 21 Or *righteousness*

³⁰There is no wisdom, no insight, no plan
    that can succeed against the LORD.

³¹The horse is made ready for the day of battle,
    but victory rests with the LORD.

REFLECTION

on **PROVERBS 21:1–2**

The heart matters. This place at the center of our being—the thoughts and feelings we have, the motives that fuel us, the dreams and desires we nurture—is extremely important to God. Many religions focus on their adherents' behaviors and the consequent outcomes: doing the right thing and producing results for their deity or their cause. But God goes deeper; a relationship with him transforms our hearts and reshapes them throughout the course of our lives.

God is interested in what we do, but the motives behind what we do are more important. Paul wrote that even profound and fruitful ministry is nothing if it isn't motivated by love (see 1 Corinthians 13:1–3). Our decisions are not hidden from God's sight; he sees every hint of every motive—usually a complicated mixture—that goes into them. So what do we do if our motives fall short of his desires? God not only can channel the hearts of kings (see Proverbs 21:1), he can shape ours. He not only sees the problem, he is the solution. We can ask the one who weighs our motives to transform them.   ♣

day**22**

22 A good name is more desirable than great riches;
to be esteemed is better than silver or gold.

² Rich and poor have this in common:
The Lord is the Maker of them all.

³ The prudent see danger and take refuge,
but the simple keep going and pay the penalty.

⁴ Humility is the fear of the Lord;
its wages are riches and honor and life.

⁵ In the paths of the wicked are snares and pitfalls,
but those who would preserve their life stay far from them.

⁶ Start children off on the way they should go,
and even when they are old they will not turn from it.

⁷ The rich rule over the poor,
and the borrower is slave to the lender.

⁸ Whoever sows injustice reaps calamity,
and the rod they wield in fury will be broken.

⁹ The generous will themselves be blessed,
for they share their food with the poor.

¹⁰ Drive out the mocker, and out goes strife;
quarrels and insults are ended.

¹¹ One who loves a pure heart and who speaks with grace
will have the king for a friend.

¹² The eyes of the Lord keep watch over knowledge,
but he frustrates the words of the unfaithful.

¹³ The sluggard says, "There's a lion outside!
I'll be killed in the public square!"

¹⁴ The mouth of an adulterous woman is a deep pit;
a man who is under the Lord's wrath falls into it.

¹⁵ Folly is bound up in the heart of a child,
    but the rod of discipline will drive it far away.

¹⁶ One who oppresses the poor to increase his wealth
    and one who gives gifts to the rich—both come to poverty.

Thirty Sayings of the Wise

Saying 1
¹⁷ Pay attention and turn your ear to the sayings of the wise;
    apply your heart to what I teach,
¹⁸ for it is pleasing when you keep them in your heart
    and have all of them ready on your lips.
¹⁹ So that your trust may be in the LORD,
    I teach you today, even you.
²⁰ Have I not written thirty sayings for you,
    sayings of counsel and knowledge,
²¹ teaching you to be honest and to speak the truth,
    so that you bring back truthful reports
    to those you serve?

Saying 2
²² Do not exploit the poor because they are poor
    and do not crush the needy in court,
²³ for the LORD will take up their case
    and will exact life for life.

Saying 3
²⁴ Do not make friends with a hot-tempered person,
    do not associate with one easily angered,
²⁵ or you may learn their ways
    and get yourself ensnared.

Saying 4
²⁶ Do not be one who shakes hands in pledge
    or puts up security for debts;
²⁷ if you lack the means to pay,
    your very bed will be snatched from under you.

Saying 5
²⁸ Do not move an ancient boundary stone
    set up by your ancestors.

Saying 6

²⁹ Do you see someone skilled in their work?

    They will serve before kings;

    they will not serve before officials of low rank.

REFLECTION

on **PROVERBS 22:29**

Years ago, "commitment to excellence" became a catchy phrase and integral part of the mission statement of many organizations. It has waned somewhat in popularity, probably for a couple of reasons: It's easy to say but hard to execute, and it shouldn't be such an unusual goal that we have to declare it. But in spite of the fact that everyone should aim for excellence without having to say so, we still see approaches to business and to personal life that ignore that standard. Some people and organizations demonstrate a commitment to just getting by, a commitment to mere survival, a commitment to just "putting in the time." Excellence is not the result.

God's people should make excellence a part of their personal ethos. It's different than striving for perfection, which produces anxiety and leads to unrealistic goals. Including excellence in our personal mission statement is something that will serve us well in our journey on earth. God honors and promotes those whose excellence — in any area of life — reflects the excellence of his name.   ✤

day23

Saying 7

23 When you sit to dine with a ruler,
note well what[a] is before you,
[2] and put a knife to your throat
if you are given to gluttony.
[3] Do not crave his delicacies,
for that food is deceptive.

Saying 8

[4] Do not wear yourself out to get rich;
do not trust your own cleverness.
[5] Cast but a glance at riches, and they are gone,
for they will surely sprout wings
and fly off to the sky like an eagle.

Saying 9

[6] Do not eat the food of a begrudging host,
do not crave his delicacies;
[7] for he is the kind of person
who is always thinking about the cost.[b]
"Eat and drink," he says to you,
but his heart is not with you.
[8] You will vomit up the little you have eaten
and will have wasted your compliments.

Saying 10

[9] Do not speak to fools,
for they will scorn your prudent words.

Saying 11

[10] Do not move an ancient boundary stone
or encroach on the fields of the fatherless,
[11] for their Defender is strong;
he will take up their case against you.

---

[a] 1 Or *who*   [b] 7 Or *for as he thinks within himself, / so he is*; or *for as he puts on a feast, / so he is*

Saying 12

¹² Apply your heart to instruction
   and your ears to words of knowledge.

Saying 13

¹³ Do not withhold discipline from a child;
   if you punish them with the rod, they will not die.
¹⁴ Punish them with the rod
   and save them from death.

Saying 14

¹⁵ My son, if your heart is wise,
   then my heart will be glad indeed;
¹⁶ my inmost being will rejoice
   when your lips speak what is right.

Saying 15

¹⁷ Do not let your heart envy sinners,
   but always be zealous for the fear of the LORD.
¹⁸ There is surely a future hope for you,
   and your hope will not be cut off.

Saying 16

¹⁹ Listen, my son, and be wise,
   and set your heart on the right path:
²⁰ Do not join those who drink too much wine
   or gorge themselves on meat,
²¹ for drunkards and gluttons become poor,
   and drowsiness clothes them in rags.

Saying 17

²² Listen to your father, who gave you life,
   and do not despise your mother when she is old.
²³ Buy the truth and do not sell it—
   wisdom, instruction and insight as well.
²⁴ The father of a righteous child has great joy;
   a man who fathers a wise son rejoices in him.
²⁵ May your father and mother rejoice;
   may she who gave you birth be joyful!

Saying 18

²⁶ My son, give me your heart
   and let your eyes delight in my ways,
²⁷ for an adulterous woman is a deep pit,
   and a wayward wife is a narrow well.
²⁸ Like a bandit she lies in wait
   and multiplies the unfaithful among men.

Saying 19

²⁹ Who has woe? Who has sorrow?
   Who has strife? Who has complaints?
   Who has needless bruises? Who has bloodshot eyes?
³⁰ Those who linger over wine,
   who go to sample bowls of mixed wine.
³¹ Do not gaze at wine when it is red,
   when it sparkles in the cup,
   when it goes down smoothly!
³² In the end it bites like a snake
   and poisons like a viper.
³³ Your eyes will see strange sights,
   and your mind will imagine confusing things.
³⁴ You will be like one sleeping on the high seas,
   lying on top of the rigging.
³⁵ "They hit me," you will say, "but I'm not hurt!
   They beat me, but I don't feel it!
  When will I wake up
   so I can find another drink?"

REFLECTION

on **PROVERBS 23:17–18**

The writer of Psalm 73 was alarmed that the wicked seemed to be having a great time in life and the righteous seemed to be suffering. That didn't fit the picture of God's justice—until the psalmist came into God's presence and got an eternal perspective (see Psalm 73:17). He realized that in the long run, the pleasures of the wicked will pass into pain and the pain of those who love God will give way to pleasures in his presence forever. The momentary view was deceptive.

That's why Proverbs strongly warns us here and elsewhere (see Proverbs 3:31; 24:1–2,19–20) against envying those who are not living for God. At times it may look like they are having all the fun, but their lives will ultimately be unfulfilling unless they forsake evil and follow God's paths. Because we are confident in our hope, we can be zealous for God and refuse to envy sinners. We are rich in God's goodness not only now but also in the future. We will never regret the hard choices we make for him.   ❖

day24

24 Do not envy the wicked,
do not desire their company;
² for their hearts plot violence,
and their lips talk about making trouble.

Saying 21

³ By wisdom a house is built,
and through understanding it is established;
⁴ through knowledge its rooms are filled
with rare and beautiful treasures.

Saying 22

⁵ The wise prevail through great power,
and those who have knowledge muster their strength.
⁶ Surely you need guidance to wage war,
and victory is won through many advisers.

Saying 23

⁷ Wisdom is too high for fools;
in the assembly at the gate they must not open their mouths.

Saying 24

⁸ Whoever plots evil
will be known as a schemer.
⁹ The schemes of folly are sin,
and people detest a mocker.

Saying 25

¹⁰ If you falter in a time of trouble,
how small is your strength!
¹¹ Rescue those being led away to death;
hold back those staggering toward slaughter.
¹² If you say, "But we knew nothing about this,"
does not he who weighs the heart perceive it?
Does not he who guards your life know it?
Will he not repay everyone according to what they have done?

Saying 26

¹³ Eat honey, my son, for it is good;
   honey from the comb is sweet to your taste.
¹⁴ Know also that wisdom is like honey for you:
   If you find it, there is a future hope for you,
   and your hope will not be cut off.

Saying 27

¹⁵ Do not lurk like a thief near the house of the righteous,
   do not plunder their dwelling place;
¹⁶ for though the righteous fall seven times, they rise again,
   but the wicked stumble when calamity strikes.

Saying 28

¹⁷ Do not gloat when your enemy falls;
   when they stumble, do not let your heart rejoice,
¹⁸ or the LORD will see and disapprove
   and turn his wrath away from them.

Saying 29

¹⁹ Do not fret because of evildoers
   or be envious of the wicked,
²⁰ for the evildoer has no future hope,
   and the lamp of the wicked will be snuffed out.

Saying 30

²¹ Fear the LORD and the king, my son,
   and do not join with rebellious officials,
²² for those two will send sudden destruction on them,
   and who knows what calamities they can bring?

Further Sayings of the Wise

²³ These also are sayings of the wise:

To show partiality in judging is not good:
²⁴ Whoever says to the guilty, "You are innocent,"
   will be cursed by peoples and denounced by nations.
²⁵ But it will go well with those who convict the guilty,
   and rich blessing will come on them.

²⁶ An honest answer
   is like a kiss on the lips.

²⁷ Put your outdoor work in order
  and get your fields ready;
  after that, build your house.

²⁸ Do not testify against your neighbor without cause—
  would you use your lips to mislead?
²⁹ Do not say, "I'll do to them as they have done to me;
  I'll pay them back for what they did."

³⁰ I went past the field of a sluggard,
  past the vineyard of someone who has no sense;
³¹ thorns had come up everywhere,
  the ground was covered with weeds,
  and the stone wall was in ruins.
³² I applied my heart to what I observed
  and learned a lesson from what I saw:
³³ A little sleep, a little slumber,
  a little folding of the hands to rest—
³⁴ and poverty will come on you like a thief
  and scarcity like an armed man.

REFLECTION

on **PROVERBS 24:30–34**

Several passages in the book of Proverbs advocate strongly for diligence and contain harsh words against laziness (see also Proverbs 6:6–11; 19:15; 26:13–16). Solomon's own work ethic was demonstrated by the massive temple and palace—not to mention Jerusalem's wall and many fortress towns throughout Israel—that were built over the course of his reign. The king accomplished a lot. But he also wore out his people, who pleaded with his successor for relief from heavy taxation and conscription of labor forces.

Hard work is good, right and godly. Being a workaholic isn't. Wisdom discerns the difference. And though laziness is condemned, the ability to rest at appropriate times is necessary—and, coincidentally, written into God's law in the form of a seventh-day Sabbath. Modern cultures are a strange mix of two extremes. Many people are far too casual about their responsibilities, while others are much too busy to take care of themselves. We need balance, working hard when it's time to work and resting well when it's time to rest. Too much of one and not enough of the other lead to ruin.   ✤

day25

More Proverbs of Solomon

25 These are more proverbs of Solomon, compiled by the men of Hezekiah king of Judah:

²It is the glory of God to conceal a matter;
   to search out a matter is the glory of kings.
³As the heavens are high and the earth is deep,
   so the hearts of kings are unsearchable.

⁴Remove the dross from the silver,
   and a silversmith can produce a vessel;
⁵remove wicked officials from the king's presence,
   and his throne will be established through righteousness.

⁶Do not exalt yourself in the king's presence,
   and do not claim a place among his great men;
⁷it is better for him to say to you, "Come up here,"
   than for him to humiliate you before his nobles.

What you have seen with your eyes
⁸   do not bring*ᵃ* hastily to court,
for what will you do in the end
   if your neighbor puts you to shame?

⁹If you take your neighbor to court,
   do not betray another's confidence,
¹⁰or the one who hears it may shame you
   and the charge against you will stand.

¹¹Like apples*ᵇ* of gold in settings of silver
   is a ruling rightly given.
¹²Like an earring of gold or an ornament of fine gold
   is the rebuke of a wise judge to a listening ear.

ᵃ 7,8 Or *nobles / on whom you had set your eyes. /⁸Do not go*
ᵇ 11 Or possibly *apricots*

¹³ Like a snow-cooled drink at harvest time
    is a trustworthy messenger to the one who sends him;
    he refreshes the spirit of his master.
¹⁴ Like clouds and wind without rain
    is one who boasts of gifts never given.

¹⁵ Through patience a ruler can be persuaded,
    and a gentle tongue can break a bone.

¹⁶ If you find honey, eat just enough—
    too much of it, and you will vomit.
¹⁷ Seldom set foot in your neighbor's house—
    too much of you, and they will hate you.

¹⁸ Like a club or a sword or a sharp arrow
    is one who gives false testimony against a neighbor.
¹⁹ Like a broken tooth or a lame foot
    is reliance on the unfaithful in a time of trouble.
²⁰ Like one who takes away a garment on a cold day,
    or like vinegar poured on a wound,
    is one who sings songs to a heavy heart.

²¹ If your enemy is hungry, give him food to eat;
    if he is thirsty, give him water to drink.
²² In doing this, you will heap burning coals on his head,
    and the LORD will reward you.

²³ Like a north wind that brings unexpected rain
    is a sly tongue—which provokes a horrified look.

²⁴ Better to live on a corner of the roof
    than share a house with a quarrelsome wife.

²⁵ Like cold water to a weary soul
    is good news from a distant land.
²⁶ Like a muddied spring or a polluted well
    are the righteous who give way to the wicked.

²⁷ It is not good to eat too much honey,
    nor is it honorable to search out matters that are too deep.

²⁸ Like a city whose walls are broken through
    is a person who lacks self-control.

REFLECTION

on **PROVERBS 25:2**

God gets glory because humans cannot fully understand his universe or the way he rules it, whereas a king gets glory if he can uncover the truth and administer justice. That can be frustrating for all of us— who, as members of God's "royal priesthood" (1 Peter 2:9), qualify in some sense for the king's privilege. But this is how God separates those who love him from those who are just curious.

Hebrews 11:6 tells us that God "rewards those who earnestly seek him." That tells us (1) that he is hard enough to find that we need to seek diligently and (2) that it won't—ultimately—be a frustrating search. In fact, this is not only the dynamic of knowing him, it's the dynamic of faith in general. God seems to enjoy the hide-and-seek nature of the relationship. He hides his treasures so that only those who know his goodness well enough to persist in faith will find them, but not so well that they are impossible to find. The whole search-and-find process is designed to draw us into a closer relationship with him.   ✣

day 26

26 Like snow in summer or rain in harvest,
  honor is not fitting for a fool.
²Like a fluttering sparrow or a darting swallow,
  an undeserved curse does not come to rest.
³A whip for the horse, a bridle for the donkey,
  and a rod for the backs of fools!
⁴Do not answer a fool according to his folly,
  or you yourself will be just like him.
⁵Answer a fool according to his folly,
  or he will be wise in his own eyes.
⁶Sending a message by the hands of a fool
  is like cutting off one's feet or drinking poison.
⁷Like the useless legs of one who is lame
  is a proverb in the mouth of a fool.
⁸Like tying a stone in a sling
  is the giving of honor to a fool.
⁹Like a thornbush in a drunkard's hand
  is a proverb in the mouth of a fool.
¹⁰Like an archer who wounds at random
  is one who hires a fool or any passer-by.
¹¹As a dog returns to its vomit,
  so fools repeat their folly.
¹²Do you see a person wise in their own eyes?
  There is more hope for a fool than for them.

¹³A sluggard says, "There's a lion in the road,
  a fierce lion roaming the streets!"
¹⁴As a door turns on its hinges,
  so a sluggard turns on his bed.
¹⁵A sluggard buries his hand in the dish;
  he is too lazy to bring it back to his mouth.
¹⁶A sluggard is wiser in his own eyes
  than seven people who answer discreetly.

¹⁷Like one who grabs a stray dog by the ears
  is someone who rushes into a quarrel not their own.

¹⁸ Like a maniac shooting
  flaming arrows of death
¹⁹ is one who deceives their neighbor
  and says, "I was only joking!"

²⁰ Without wood a fire goes out;
  without a gossip a quarrel dies down.
²¹ As charcoal to embers and as wood to fire,
  so is a quarrelsome person for kindling strife.
²² The words of a gossip are like choice morsels;
  they go down to the inmost parts.

²³ Like a coating of silver dross on earthenware
  are fervent[a] lips with an evil heart.
²⁴ Enemies disguise themselves with their lips,
  but in their hearts they harbor deceit.
²⁵ Though their speech is charming, do not believe them,
  for seven abominations fill their hearts.
²⁶ Their malice may be concealed by deception,
  but their wickedness will be exposed in the assembly.
²⁷ Whoever digs a pit will fall into it;
  if someone rolls a stone, it will roll back on them.
²⁸ A lying tongue hates those it hurts,
  and a flattering mouth works ruin.

[a] 23 Hebrew; Septuagint *smooth*

REFLECTION

on **PROVERBS 26:4–5**

Though Proverbs 26:4 and 5 appear at first to be contradictory, two different situations are being addressed. To get into an argument with a fool makes one look like a fool. But sometimes folly must be exposed and denounced. Plus, the one who rebukes the fool discourages the person from becoming proud. In insignificant issues, we should just ignore foolish persons; in issues that matter, they must be dealt with because others may be led astray by their words.

God's Word is thoroughly consistent, yet some directions given for certain situations and seasons in our lives may seem contradictory. For example, when faced with a huge decision, do we wait on the Lord or move forward in faith? Both options are encouraged in Scripture, but only one fits a particular moment. Do we save some of our resources for the future or lay up our treasures in heaven rather than on earth? Both are Biblical principles, but principles are never enough. God has not called us into a relationship with principles; he has called us into a relationship with him. In any given situation, we need to bring our circumstances to him and listen for his response. ✣

day27

27 Do not boast about tomorrow,
for you do not know what a day may bring.

² Let someone else praise you, and not your own mouth;
an outsider, and not your own lips.

³ Stone is heavy and sand a burden,
but a fool's provocation is heavier than both.

⁴ Anger is cruel and fury overwhelming,
but who can stand before jealousy?

⁵ Better is open rebuke
than hidden love.

⁶ Wounds from a friend can be trusted,
but an enemy multiplies kisses.

⁷ One who is full loathes honey from the comb,
but to the hungry even what is bitter tastes sweet.

⁸ Like a bird that flees its nest
is anyone who flees from home.

⁹ Perfume and incense bring joy to the heart,
and the pleasantness of a friend
springs from their heartfelt advice.

¹⁰ Do not forsake your friend or a friend of your family,
and do not go to your relative's house when disaster strikes
you—
better a neighbor nearby than a relative far away.

¹¹ Be wise, my son, and bring joy to my heart;
then I can answer anyone who treats me with contempt.

¹² The prudent see danger and take refuge,
but the simple keep going and pay the penalty.

¹³ Take the garment of one who puts up security for a stranger;
   hold it in pledge if it is done for an outsider.

¹⁴ If anyone loudly blesses their neighbor early in the morning,
   it will be taken as a curse.

¹⁵ A quarrelsome wife is like the dripping
   of a leaky roof in a rainstorm;
¹⁶ restraining her is like restraining the wind
   or grasping oil with the hand.

¹⁷ As iron sharpens iron,
   so one person sharpens another.

¹⁸ The one who guards a fig tree will eat its fruit,
   and whoever protects their master will be honored.

¹⁹ As water reflects the face,
   so one's life reflects the heart.[a]

²⁰ Death and Destruction[b] are never satisfied,
   and neither are human eyes.

²¹ The crucible for silver and the furnace for gold,
   but people are tested by their praise.

²² Though you grind a fool in a mortar,
   grinding them like grain with a pestle,
   you will not remove their folly from them.

²³ Be sure you know the condition of your flocks,
   give careful attention to your herds;
²⁴ for riches do not endure forever,
   and a crown is not secure for all generations.
²⁵ When the hay is removed and new growth appears
   and the grass from the hills is gathered in,
²⁶ the lambs will provide you with clothing,
   and the goats with the price of a field.
²⁷ You will have plenty of goats' milk to feed your family
   and to nourish your female servants.

---

a 19 Or so others reflect your heart back to you   *b 20 Hebrew Abaddon*

DAY 2778

on **PROVERBS 27:5–6,9**

Some people love a good fight. Most, however, avoid conflict whenever possible. There's a healthy balance between contentiousness and
conflict avoidance, and finding that balance can be very rewarding
in the context of relationships. As those who are called to speak the
truth in love (see Ephesians 4:15), we need to be open to both giving
and receiving hard advice with those we care about. The wounds from
a friend are far better than flattery from an enemy. Heartfelt counsel,
even if it isn't what we want to say or hear, is worth a lot.

It's hard to be completely honest in confronting someone because
we risk rejection if the honesty isn't well received. And it's hard to be
on the receiving end because we can easily mistake constructive criti-
cism for disapproval or rejection. But this is part of how "iron sharpens
iron" (Proverbs 27:17). We become stronger in relationships in which
blunt honesty flourishes without being threatening. We need to be
strong enough to speak truth into the lives of those close to us—and
to allow them to speak truth into ours.   ✤

day28

28 The wicked flee though no one pursues,
but the righteous are as bold as a lion.

[2] When a country is rebellious, it has many rulers,
but a ruler with discernment and knowledge maintains order.

[3] A ruler[a] who oppresses the poor
is like a driving rain that leaves no crops.

[4] Those who forsake instruction praise the wicked,
but those who heed it resist them.

[5] Evildoers do not understand what is right,
but those who seek the LORD understand it fully.

[6] Better the poor whose walk is blameless
than the rich whose ways are perverse.

[7] A discerning son heeds instruction,
but a companion of gluttons disgraces his father.

[8] Whoever increases wealth by taking interest or profit from the
poor
amasses it for another, who will be kind to the poor.

[9] If anyone turns a deaf ear to my instruction,
even their prayers are detestable.

[10] Whoever leads the upright along an evil path
will fall into their own trap,
but the blameless will receive a good inheritance.

[11] The rich are wise in their own eyes;
one who is poor and discerning sees how deluded they are.

[12] When the righteous triumph, there is great elation;
but when the wicked rise to power, people go into hiding.

[13] Whoever conceals their sins does not prosper,
but the one who confesses and renounces them finds mercy.

[a] 3 Or *A poor person*

¹⁴Blessed is the one who always trembles before God,
    but whoever hardens their heart falls into trouble.

¹⁵Like a roaring lion or a charging bear
    is a wicked ruler over a helpless people.

¹⁶A tyrannical ruler practices extortion,
    but one who hates ill-gotten gain will enjoy a long reign.

¹⁷Anyone tormented by the guilt of murder
    will seek refuge in the grave;
    let no one hold them back.

¹⁸The one whose walk is blameless is kept safe,
    but the one whose ways are perverse will fall into the pit.[a]

¹⁹Those who work their land will have abundant food,
    but those who chase fantasies will have their fill of poverty.

²⁰A faithful person will be richly blessed,
    but one eager to get rich will not go unpunished.

²¹To show partiality is not good—
    yet a person will do wrong for a piece of bread.

²²The stingy are eager to get rich
    and are unaware that poverty awaits them.

²³Whoever rebukes a person will in the end gain favor
    rather than one who has a flattering tongue.

²⁴Whoever robs their father or mother
    and says, "It's not wrong,"
    is partner to one who destroys.

²⁵The greedy stir up conflict,
    but those who trust in the Lord will prosper.

²⁶Those who trust in themselves are fools,
    but those who walk in wisdom are kept safe.

²⁷Those who give to the poor will lack nothing,
    but those who close their eyes to them receive many curses.

²⁸When the wicked rise to power, people go into hiding;
    but when the wicked perish, the righteous thrive.

[a] 18 Syriac (see Septuagint); Hebrew *into one*

REFLECTION

on **PROVERBS 28:27**

God is a generous God, and his people are to be generous people. "Freely you have received; freely give," Jesus told his disciples (Matthew 10:8). That concept applies to every area of life. Paul tells us that "God loves a cheerful giver" (2 Corinthians 9:7). Throughout Scripture, we are encouraged to live with an open hand. Why? Because God opens his hand to us.

That's why so many verses in Proverbs and in the rest of the Bible warn of the dangers of greed. It isn't wealth that's wrong—God gave quite a few of his choice servants in Scripture an abundance of possessions. But the pursuit of wealth as a goal can be dangerous, distracting from God's purposes and tempting us to sin. Material poverty cultivates a much truer spiritual perspective than greed does, but the rich who give generously have a true spiritual perspective—and the means to do a lot of good. God blesses those who, like him, live with an open hand. ✣

day29

29 Whoever remains stiff-necked after many rebukes
will suddenly be destroyed—without remedy.

² When the righteous thrive, the people rejoice;
when the wicked rule, the people groan.

³ A man who loves wisdom brings joy to his father,
but a companion of prostitutes squanders his wealth.

⁴ By justice a king gives a country stability,
but those who are greedy for*ᵃ* bribes tear it down.

⁵ Those who flatter their neighbors
are spreading nets for their feet.

⁶ Evildoers are snared by their own sin,
but the righteous shout for joy and are glad.

⁷ The righteous care about justice for the poor,
but the wicked have no such concern.

⁸ Mockers stir up a city,
but the wise turn away anger.

⁹ If a wise person goes to court with a fool,
the fool rages and scoffs, and there is no peace.

¹⁰ The bloodthirsty hate a person of integrity
and seek to kill the upright.

¹¹ Fools give full vent to their rage,
but the wise bring calm in the end.

¹² If a ruler listens to lies,
all his officials become wicked.

¹³ The poor and the oppressor have this in common:
The LORD gives sight to the eyes of both.

ᵃ 4 Or *who give*

¹⁴If a king judges the poor with fairness,
    his throne will be established forever.

¹⁵A rod and a reprimand impart wisdom,
    but a child left undisciplined disgraces its mother.

¹⁶When the wicked thrive, so does sin,
    but the righteous will see their downfall.

¹⁷Discipline your children, and they will give you peace;
    they will bring you the delights you desire.

¹⁸Where there is no revelation, people cast off restraint;
    but blessed is the one who heeds wisdom's instruction.

¹⁹Servants cannot be corrected by mere words;
    though they understand, they will not respond.

²⁰Do you see someone who speaks in haste?
    There is more hope for a fool than for them.

²¹A servant pampered from youth
    will turn out to be insolent.

²²An angry person stirs up conflict,
    and a hot-tempered person commits many sins.

²³Pride brings a person low,
    but the lowly in spirit gain honor.

²⁴The accomplices of thieves are their own enemies;
    they are put under oath and dare not testify.

²⁵Fear of man will prove to be a snare,
    but whoever trusts in the LORD is kept safe.

²⁶Many seek an audience with a ruler,
    but it is from the LORD that one gets justice.

²⁷The righteous detest the dishonest;
    the wicked detest the upright.

REFLECTION

on **PROVERBS 29:25**

The Gospel of Luke tells us that the Jewish religious leaders wanted to get rid of Jesus because "they were afraid of the people" (Luke 22:2). Fear of losing their influence and of the consequences of social unrest fueled their hatred of Jesus and contributed to their desire to have him put to death. We have our own fears, usually less dramatic—loss of security, position, influence, approval, reputation, income and much more—and we make compromises we know we shouldn't make.

Our fears usually prove to be a snare for us, and they all stem from not trusting God. Fear is behind peer pressure, compromise, an unbridled pursuit of wealth and security, and much of what we do for affirmation and approval. Fear diverts us from an uncompromising commitment to God and his plan for our lives. The remedy is trust: a choice to depend entirely on God for all we need in every area of life. When we trust him completely, no one can intimidate us. We are free to live as he wants us to live.   ❖

day 30

Sayings of Agur

30 The sayings of Agur son of Jakeh—an inspired utterance.

This man's utterance to Ithiel:

"I am weary, God,
  but I can prevail.[a]
² Surely I am only a brute, not a man;
  I do not have human understanding.
³ I have not learned wisdom,
  nor have I attained to the knowledge of the Holy One.
⁴ Who has gone up to heaven and come down?
  Whose hands have gathered up the wind?
 Who has wrapped up the waters in a cloak?
  Who has established all the ends of the earth?
 What is his name, and what is the name of his son?
  Surely you know!

⁵ "Every word of God is flawless;
  he is a shield to those who take refuge in him.
⁶ Do not add to his words,
  or he will rebuke you and prove you a liar.

⁷ "Two things I ask of you, Lord;
  do not refuse me before I die:
⁸ Keep falsehood and lies far from me;
  give me neither poverty nor riches,
  but give me only my daily bread.
⁹ Otherwise, I may have too much and disown you
  and say, 'Who is the Lord?'
 Or I may become poor and steal,
  and so dishonor the name of my God.

¹⁰ "Do not slander a servant to their master,
  or they will curse you, and you will pay for it.

---

a 1 With a different word division of the Hebrew; Masoretic Text *utterance to Ithiel, / to Ithiel and Ukal:*

11 "There are those who curse their fathers
    and do not bless their mothers;
12 those who are pure in their own eyes
    and yet are not cleansed of their filth;
13 those whose eyes are ever so haughty,
    whose glances are so disdainful;
14 those whose teeth are swords
    and whose jaws are set with knives
to devour the poor from the earth
    and the needy from among mankind.

15 "The leech has two daughters.
    'Give! Give!' they cry.

    "There are three things that are never satisfied,
        four that never say, 'Enough!':
16 the grave, the barren womb,
    land, which is never satisfied with water,
    and fire, which never says, 'Enough!'

17 "The eye that mocks a father,
    that scorns an aged mother,
will be pecked out by the ravens of the valley,
    will be eaten by the vultures.

18 "There are three things that are too amazing for me,
    four that I do not understand:
19 the way of an eagle in the sky,
    the way of a snake on a rock,
the way of a ship on the high seas,
    and the way of a man with a young woman.

20 "This is the way of an adulterous woman:
    She eats and wipes her mouth
    and says, 'I've done nothing wrong.'

21 "Under three things the earth trembles,
    under four it cannot bear up:
22 a servant who becomes king,
    a godless fool who gets plenty to eat,
23 a contemptible woman who gets married,
    and a servant who displaces her mistress.

24 "Four things on earth are small,
    yet they are extremely wise:

²⁵ Ants are creatures of little strength,
    yet they store up their food in the summer;
²⁶ hyraxes are creatures of little power,
    yet they make their home in the crags;
²⁷ locusts have no king,
    yet they advance together in ranks;
²⁸ a lizard can be caught with the hand,
    yet it is found in kings' palaces.

²⁹ "There are three things that are stately in their stride,
    four that move with stately bearing:
³⁰ a lion, mighty among beasts,
    who retreats before nothing;
³¹ a strutting rooster, a he-goat,
    and a king secure against revolt.[a]

³² "If you play the fool and exalt yourself,
    or if you plan evil,
    clap your hand over your mouth!
³³ For as churning cream produces butter,
    and as twisting the nose produces blood,
    so stirring up anger produces strife."

[a] 31 The meaning of the Hebrew for this phrase is uncertain.

REFLECTION

on PROVERBS 30:15-31

The sayings of Agur are an exercise in how to find truth in the living parables God has put around us. In nature and human society, Agur found pictures of dissatisfaction, untraceable mysteries, unbearable people, wisdom in small packages and confident attitudes. There's nothing particularly remarkable in these images, but the fact that Agur seemed to be interacting with God through the visuals around him is remarkable. We see this often in Scripture—God speaking in pictures rather than words. For example, God gave us visual illustrations in the tabernacle and in its articles of worship. God's preferred language seems to be images.

It helps to know that, especially when we're listening for God to speak in the depths of our spirits. If we're only tuning in to hear words, we might miss something. God surrounds us with living parables—natural or social illustrations of spiritual truth. If we ask him to show us lessons in life, we will begin to "see" his voice more often. ❖

day31

Sayings of King Lemuel

31 The sayings of King Lemuel—an inspired utterance his mother taught him.

² Listen, my son! Listen, son of my womb!
　　Listen, my son, the answer to my prayers!
³ Do not spend your strength*a* on women,
　　your vigor on those who ruin kings.

⁴ It is not for kings, Lemuel—
　　it is not for kings to drink wine,
　　not for rulers to crave beer,
⁵ lest they drink and forget what has been decreed,
　　and deprive all the oppressed of their rights.
⁶ Let beer be for those who are perishing,
　　wine for those who are in anguish!
⁷ Let them drink and forget their poverty
　　and remember their misery no more.

⁸ Speak up for those who cannot speak for themselves,
　　for the rights of all who are destitute.
⁹ Speak up and judge fairly;
　　defend the rights of the poor and needy.

Epilogue: The Wife of Noble Character

¹⁰ *b* A wife of noble character who can find?
　　She is worth far more than rubies.
¹¹ Her husband has full confidence in her
　　and lacks nothing of value.
¹² She brings him good, not harm,
　　all the days of her life.

---

a 3 Or *wealth*　　*b 10* Verses 10-31 are an acrostic poem, the verses of which begin with the successive letters of the Hebrew alphabet.

¹³ She selects wool and flax
 and works with eager hands.
¹⁴ She is like the merchant ships,
 bringing her food from afar.
¹⁵ She gets up while it is still night;
 she provides food for her family
 and portions for her female servants.
¹⁶ She considers a field and buys it;
 out of her earnings she plants a vineyard.
¹⁷ She sets about her work vigorously;
 her arms are strong for her tasks.
¹⁸ She sees that her trading is profitable,
 and her lamp does not go out at night.
¹⁹ In her hand she holds the distaff
 and grasps the spindle with her fingers.
²⁰ She opens her arms to the poor
 and extends her hands to the needy.
²¹ When it snows, she has no fear for her household;
 for all of them are clothed in scarlet.
²² She makes coverings for her bed;
 she is clothed in fine linen and purple.
²³ Her husband is respected at the city gate,
 where he takes his seat among the elders of the land.
²⁴ She makes linen garments and sells them,
 and supplies the merchants with sashes.
²⁵ She is clothed with strength and dignity;
 she can laugh at the days to come.
²⁶ She speaks with wisdom,
 and faithful instruction is on her tongue.
²⁷ She watches over the affairs of her household
 and does not eat the bread of idleness.
²⁸ Her children arise and call her blessed;
 her husband also, and he praises her:
²⁹ "Many women do noble things,
 but you surpass them all."
³⁰ Charm is deceptive, and beauty is fleeting;
 but a woman who fears the LORD is to be praised.
³¹ Honor her for all that her hands have done,
 and let her works bring her praise at the city gate.

REFLECTION

on PROVERBS 31:10–31

The book of Proverbs ends with a dazzling description of "a wife of noble character" (Proverbs 31:10). She does everything well. She takes care of her home, works with her hands, buys a field and tends it, gets up early and stays up late, trades like a savvy merchant, meets all the needs of the family, works with charities and earns the admiration of everyone around her. This woman is more valuable than priceless jewels.

The problem is that no woman can fit this profile. Some may approach this ideal, but it's hard to imagine anyone with this degree of versatility, universal affirmation and freedom from conflict. It's an impossible standard for any woman.

This description is actually a composite portrayal of admirable characteristics in women—an encouraging and liberating image that has something for every woman to strive for. This poem captures the ideals of wisdom that have filled Proverbs. Most importantly, the woman in the poem fears the Lord. And, as we know, that's where wisdom begins.　　　　　　　　　　　　　　　　　　　❖

Go Deeper with *NIV Once-A-Day Bibles*

NIV Once-A-Day Bible

The *NIV Once-A-Day Bible* organizes the New International Version Bible—the world's most popular modern-English Bible—into 365 daily readings. This softcover edition includes a daily Scripture reading from both the Old and New Testaments, plus a Psalm or a Proverb, followed by a short devotional thought written by the staff at the trusted ministry Walk Thru the Bible.

Softcover: 978-0-310-95092-9

NIV Once-A-Day Bible: Chronological Edition

The *NIV Once-A-Day Bible: Chronological Edition* organizes the New International Version Bible—the world's most popular modern-English Bible—into 365 daily readings placed in chronological order. This softcover edition includes a daily Scripture reading followed by a short devotional thought written by the staff at the trusted ministry Walk Thru the Bible.

Softcover: 978-0-310-95095-0

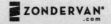

Once-A-Day Devotional for Women

This devotional book is designed with 365 daily readings created specifically for women. Using devotions from Livingstone, the group who produced the *Life Application Study Bible*, each daily reading includes a Scripture passage to read, a devotion on that passage, a prayer, plus additional Scriptures to explore.

Softcover: 978-0-310-44072-7

Once-A-Day Walk with Jesus Devotional

The *Once-A-Day Walk with Jesus Devotional* introduces you to the New Testament of the Bible through 365 daily readings, allowing you to read through the New Testament in one year. With devotions created by the trusted ministry Walk Thru the Bible, each reading offers unique ways to center on God and strengthen your faith: by reading a Scripture portion, followed by an insight

from a remarkable Christian writer of the past, and ending with a timely, personal application and worship portion to help focus your prayer and lead you into a time of reflection – all centered on that day's particular focus. The quotes from past Christian writers include insights from such well-known authors as John Calvin, Dwight L. Moody, Hannah Whitall Smith, Martin Luther, Charles Spurgeon, and many others.

Softcover: 978-0-310-44324-7